Praise for

DRIVEN TO DELIVER

The opportunity to peer into the life of one who has gained important leadership wisdom is a rare treat. This book is such an opportunity. Through the lens of his life's story, Harry Smith shares nine life principles that are the bedrock of his successful career. I'm grateful for the business savvy, relationship-oriented and faith-filled lessons he has taken the time to pass along. May the Lord raise up young Christian businessmen—and churchmen—to take up his legacy and mantle for the coming generation.

— THOM S. RAINER
President and CEO
LifeWay Christian Resources

This book is written at a crucial time in our current era by Harry Smith, one of few individuals that I am aware of, who is both very materially and spiritually successful. His nine principles prove the point that if one does the right thing and continues doing the right thing, one will meet with success, not only from a peace-of-mind perspective, but also financially. I am truly blessed to have known Harry. Many times when faced with difficult choices I have found myself asking, "What would Harry do?"

—RAJIV GROVER, PH.D.
Dean, Fogelman College of Business and Economics
Chair of Excellence, Sales and Marketing
University of Memphis

Praise for

DRIVEN TO DELIVER

If you ever wanted to model your life after a Christian businessman, Harry Smith is who you would follow. He has integrated his faith in the workplace, and his example has been outstanding. Harry Smith exemplifies the type of person one would aspire to be. If you knew Harry, you would love Harry. There is not a more gentle, sincere, wise, encouraging, genuine person in the world today. He is the perfect picture of faith, a husband, a father, a friend, a businessman, and now a grandfather. My days are always brighter if Harry Smith is on my calendar. He has an uncanny way of making your day better. The guy is a true life Barnabas. I have never been with Harry without him encouraging me in some way. Faith, character, and love would pretty much sum up Harry Smith. He has lived by these virtues all his life. He has impacted not only his generation, but the one above and the one below. The fruits of the Spirit come to mind when thinking about my friend Harry Smith. Not just a couple of them, but every one of them: love, joy, peace, patience, kindness, goodness, faithfulness, gentleness, self-control.

—KEMMONS WILSON, JR.
Principal, Kemmons Wilson, Inc.

Praise for

DRIVEN TO DELIVER

Leaders need wisdom. When Solomon became Israel's king, he wisely asked God for wisdom. Without wisdom, the plans of any individual, organization, or nation are doomed. Harry Smith is a man of wisdom. I've been his pastor and close friend since 2005. We have prayed together and discussed many important matters. He has helped me and many others in our church and community navigate through complex situations. That is why I am so excited about his new book, DRIVEN TO DELIVER. In this insightful work, you will discover the guiding principles of Harry's life that have helped him become such a successful Christian, husband, father, churchman, and businessman. The book you're holding is powerful. If you read and apply it, you will grow in wisdom and true success.

—STEVE GAINES, PH.D.
Senior Pastor
Bellevue Baptist Church
Memphis, Tennessee

DRIVEN TO DELIVER is a terrific work written by one of the most successful businessmen that I know. The book provides every reader with a checklist for living a centered life. I am blessed to have had Harry Smith as my friend for 20 years. I have watched this humble man of God live his nine keys for success. I recommend this book to anyone interested in living a successful, balanced life.

—R. ANDREW TAYLOR
CEO, Gerber
Taylor Capital Advisors, Inc.

Praise for

DRIVEN TO DELIVER

There are few people in this life that are a pleasure to know and are ones that you want to emulate, but Harry Smith is one of those. His book DRIVEN TO DELIVER reveals nine steps to help everyone be a true success in today's business world. As a fellow traveler and friend of Harry Smith, I have witnessed firsthand his practice of these nine steps to success and can attest that they work. He is a great example for all of us because he is a very successful businessman, a leader in the community, and a devoted follower of Jesus Christ. If you are looking for a practical guide to help you be a winner in life, this is the book for you.

—DAVID C. PERDUE
CEO
Asentinel, LLC

DRIVEN TO DELIVER

Harry L. Smith

To: Kirk

Thank you for being my friend. I Am thankful for the opportunity to serve with you. Blessings to you and your family!

HARRY

Phill. 4:6

DRIVEN TO DELIVER

Harry L. Smith

former President and CEO of Schilling Enterprises

With a foreword by *David S. Dockery*
President, Union University

BorderStone Press, LLC

2011

First American Edition

Driven to Deliver

Author: Harry L. Smith
Foreword: David S. Dockery
Editors: Andrew Taylor, Cyndi Richardson

Published by BorderStone Press, LLC, PO Box 1383, Mountain Home, AR 72654
Dallas, TX - Memphis, TN

www.borderstonepress.com

Copy editor: Dr. Roger D. Duke
Supervising editor: Brian Mooney

ISBN: 978-1-936670-39-0

Library of Congress Control Number: 2011933997

Interior is acid free and lignin free.
It meets all ANSI standards for archival quality paper.

TABLE OF CONTENTS

ACKNOWLEDGMENTS

To my wife Beth – Thank you for your love and support. We met at church as teenagers and have been together now for five decades. I am grateful that you are still my best friend.

To my daughter Leslie – Thank you for your love and patience. You are a wonderful wife to Rex and a dedicated mother to your three boys. You have many gifts and talents, and I am so proud of you!

To Rex, my son-in-law, partner, and friend – You are the best son-in-law a father could have.

To my grandsons Barrett, Harrison, and Walker – You inspired me to write this book so I could pass down the lessons I have learned to you and to others. It blesses your Papa to see you becoming fine young men. I love you very much!

To David Dockery – It has been a blessing to serve alongside with you at Union University. Thank you for your friendship and for encouraging me to publish this book.

To my friends who have supported and encouraged me over the years – Your wisdom, love, and prayers have kept me going. You know who you are!

I would also like to thank *Andrew Taylor, Kemmons Wilson, Jr., and Cyndi Richardson* who helped me with this book and others who encouraged me to complete it.

A special thank you goes *to my church family* with whom I am blessed to worship and serve.

Above all, I thank God for always being with me. Without Him, I could not have made it.

FOREWORD

BY DAVID S. DOCKERY

WISDOM IS ONE of life's great gifts, which is gained from knowledge, understanding, and the experiences of life. Wisdom is developed from keeping one's own counsel and practicing what one teaches. The book you are holding in your hands is a book of wise sayings being passed on from one generation to the next. What started out as a project to be shared with the grandsons of Harry L. Smith has now, through a variety of influences, been made available in a much broader format, for which we all can rejoice and give thanks.

Harry Smith is one of the wisest men I have ever had the privilege to know. I met this man over a dozen years ago in a providential encounter. A mutual friend had invited Harry to a meeting where I was speaking. From that introduction, he has become a cherished friend.

He now has served as a trustee at Union University, where I also serve, for about ten of those years, four of them as Chairman of the Board. The wisdom found in this book was often shared in different ways in various settings in our meetings. The Union Board of Trustees is stronger for the influence of Harry Smith, and Union University is a better institution because of his wise leadership of this group.

Harry Smith makes people around him better. He is not only a wise and encouraging counselor, but a person with high expectations. Those around him soon learn of those expectations and work to improve in all areas of life. Not only have I read this book with great benefit, but I have seen this book lived out before me and before others. My own life is better because of time spent with the author of this book. The lessons to be gained here regarding faith, family, and finances, among other things, are valuable and worthy of serious reflection. I know I have been blessed by the life and influence of Harry Smith. My prediction is that you will greatly benefit as well, as you work your way through this book.

The fascinating story of how these life lessons were gained along the way in the circumstances of Harry's life certainly provides interesting reading. The biographical account, however, merely provides the framework for the sharing of these valuable lessons. I am grateful to God that Harry Smith has been led to put these wise teachings in this format for the good of many.

I encourage you to read with both interest and discernment. While doing so, let me encourage you to think about the words from the Apostle James found in the New Testament:

If any of you lacks wisdom, he should ask God, who gives generously to all without finding fault, and it will be given to him (James 1:5 NIV).

May God grant you wisdom for life's journey and may he use the lessons found in *Driven to Deliver* to guide you on your way.

—DAVID S. DOCKERY
President, Union University

INTRODUCTION

FROM THE WINDOW of my hotel room in Henry Ford's hometown, I had an inescapable view of "The Glass House." You couldn't miss Ford Motor Company World Headquarters, a Goliath-sized structure of steel and glass, gleaming in the spring sunshine.

It was on a Wednesday in April, 1980, and I was in Dearborn, Michigan, as the new president of a company that was desperately fighting to survive. Just four months earlier I left a three-partner accounting firm in Florence, Alabama to become CEO of the Schilling companies in Memphis, Tennessee. At age 37 and with little formal leadership training, I was suddenly responsible for a business with 1,000 employees and annual revenues of $100 million.

When I took on this challenge, the global economy was bad and getting worse. Our trucking operation that delivered new Ford vehicles to dealers had suffered tremendous losses. Disregarding a 50-year working relationship, Ford abruptly decided to terminate our vehicle transport and delivery business. Against a giant international organization like Ford Motor Company, I felt like David the shepherd boy—but without a slingshot.

On Monday and Tuesday I had appealed our case, working my way through several layers of Ford hierarchy until I met with the executive vice president. The results from these meetings were more than disappointing; they were devastating. Ford was taking away our business within the next five weeks.

I was alone in my hotel room feeling anxious when the telephone rang. It was the manager of the Ford Motor Credit office in Memphis calling. I had met him for the first time a few days earlier when he came by my office. "How are things going?" he asked. I said, "Not good. It looks like we're going to lose our trucking business." After giving an update, I confided to him that if it were not for God, I didn't know how I would make it.

What this man said next convinced me that I had a weapon more powerful than any earthly arsenal could contain. He told me that he and his wife had prayed for me that morning and that they would continue to pray for me.

I hung up the phone and got down on my knees. Through tears in my eyes, I looked out at the Glass House and said, "Ford, you haven't got a chance. I don't think you have anyone praying for you, and I have people praying for me!" God's response to prayers for deliverance was a defining moment in my life.

We all need help. We can't make it by ourselves. I believe most of us encounter the same challenges in life. We tend to think our concerns are unique to us, but I don't believe that's true.

I have spent 58 years delivering newspapers, working in public accounting, real estate, automobile dealerships, trucking, and other businesses as well as not-for-profit organizations. I have had four careers, and each career came about through the relationships that I made along the way.

My original intention for starting this project was to pass along the lessons I've learned about life to my grandsons. However, in 2010, I was invited to serve as an Executive-in-Residence at the University of Memphis Fogelman School of Business and Economics. At the U of M, I had the opportunity to share my life principles with graduating seniors. It was at the U of M that Dr. Rajiv Grover, Dean of the College of Business and Economics, encouraged me to share my story with a wider audience.

Another reason for tackling this project was that earlier in 2010, Herbert Rhea, my mentor and friend of 30 years, died at the age of 87. I had promised Herb that I would pass on what he had taught me.

If you go through life with one or two good friends, you're blessed. I was blessed to have a mentor like Herbert Rhea and others who helped me. When I was inducted into the Society of Entrepreneurs, Herb introduced me to the group that evening. He said, "You never know when the next person you meet will become one of your best friends."

I'm so thankful for Herb's friendship and guidance, and through this book I pray that his influence will continue. Throughout my life I have been blessed with good role models who demonstrated in their lives that right wins over wrong. I hope the principles I share with you will encourage and help you to better balance your life.

God has blessed me with a wonderful family. My wife Beth and I have been married for 48 years. We have one daughter, Leslie. She and her husband Rex Jones have three sons: Barrett, 21; Harrison, 19; and Walker, 17. Leslie and her family live near us, so we have had the pleasure of playing a part in the lives of our grandchildren. We are all members of Bellevue Baptist Church in Cordova, Tennessee, a suburb of Memphis. Rex is a special person to me. Not only is he my son-in-law, but he has been my business partner as well. I have always said that if I could have chosen my son-in-law from anyone in the world, I would have picked Rex. We all enjoy spending time together and place great value on our family relationship.

When I speak to students at the University of Memphis, I share my nine life principles. These principles, which I describe in detail in Chapter 10, are:

1. Have a genuine interest in everything you do.
2. Improve your mind continually.
3. Live a lifestyle focused on good physical health.
4. Practice ethical standards.
5. Demonstrate a selfless attitude through humility.
6. Continually strengthen your communication skills.
7. Let your life reflect loyalty to others.
8. Develop leadership qualities.
9. Strive to finish strong.

My careers have taken me from delivering newspapers to public accounting to chief executive of a group of companies, and finally, to my current career of board service. The following chapters describe my life and how my experiences helped me develop these nine principles. They apply to each of my four careers and I believe they can apply to any career.

Looking back over my life, I can see how each career prepared me for the next step along my road. There were times when I was overwhelmed with my work, but God always helped me. I'm just an ordinary person, but He is supernatural. I give Him glory and thanks for all that He has given me.

CHAPTER ONE

MY CHILDHOOD,
FAMILY AND FIRST CAREER

I WAS BORN on December 6, 1942, in Florence, Alabama. The hospital was a block away from First Baptist Church, the church I attended most of my life until my family moved to Memphis in 1980. For several years my family and I lived three blocks from the church and five blocks from downtown Florence.

I don't remember much about my early childhood. My father was from Lawrenceburg, Tennessee, and my mother was from Florence. We lived in Columbus, Ohio, and in Lawrenceburg for a few months after I was born. We moved to Florence where I lived until 1980. Unfortunately, my father was an alcoholic and was abusive to my mother. My parents divorced when I was five years old. People find things in their lives to blame their failures on, like a

missing father. I was fortunate that my mother
made sacrifices to help me overcome this. We
became a team to provide for our family income
and to fill the void of my father's absence.

After the divorce, my mother and I lived
with my grandparents, Dempsey and Esther
Humphries. I spent a lot of time with "Mom"
and "Pop." I remember sitting around a card
table with them in the living room learning how
to play Rook, Canasta, and other card games.
My grandfather and my mother's brother Tom
owned Humphries & Son Trucking Company.
Tom lived across the street from us. My
mother's other brother, D. M., lived in Toledo,
Ohio.

Both my grandparents died when I was seven
years old. My grandmother had lung cancer,
and my grandfather died from a cerebral
hemorrhage. At the time, my mother was
working at the Flagg Utica Knitting Mill, a
clothing factory. When my grandparents died,
it was a struggle for her to work outside the
home and to care for me. So she quit her job at
the factory and earned income by renting the
two upstairs apartments and taking in boarders
downstairs. There were usually three or four
ladies living in our home while they attended

the local beautician school. My mother also rented out the house we lived in before my parents were divorced.

My first career began when I was nine years old. On my bicycle I delivered the *Birmingham News,* an afternoon paper, to 25 customers spread out over several blocks in Florence. The longest-running job I had during my school years began at age ten when my mother and I delivered an afternoon rural paper route together. We drove 40 miles every day, 365 days a year, delivering about 100 newspapers. We had paper boys who carried another 100 papers for us. When I was old enough to drive the route myself, I hired someone to help me. This rural paper route was another means of financial support for our family.

Although I may have missed a lot growing up without a father at home, my mother did her best and taught me many lessons about life. A cherished memory that I have is the two of us singing our favorite song, "Love Lifted Me," while delivering the *Birmingham News* on Sunday mornings.

When I was 13, I begged my mother for a motorcycle so that I could deliver the *Birmingham Post Herald,* a morning paper, before school. She finally agreed to let me buy a small Harley-Davidson motorcycle which cost $200. Because it was green, I named my new motorcycle "The Green Flame."

My morning paper route, which I delivered for about a year, required me to get up at 4:30 or 5:00 in the morning and head downtown to pick up my papers. As I prepared for the morning delivery, I could smell the aroma of fresh, hot donuts coming from Culpepper's Bakery which opened at 5:00 a.m. In the pre-dawn cold temperatures, the rubber bands sometimes snapped and stung my hands as I rolled them around the newspapers. I stuffed the papers in a large canvas bag and loaded it on the front of "The Green Flame."

At the time I began delivering my morning paper route, I still had my afternoon route which I continued through my senior year in college. The afternoon paper route paid my way through college. After getting up early to deliver my morning paper route in the tenth grade, I often fell asleep in my algebra class which was after lunch. I had to attend summer school that year because of bad grades.

One afternoon when I was waiting for the papers to arrive for my motor route, I had an upset stomach and needed to get home quickly. My home was ten blocks away. Because I was in such a hurry, I failed to stop at a stop sign. A police officer pulled me over. When I explained the urgency of the situation, he said he would follow me home. Afterwards, the officer gave me a ticket! Fortunately, the judge at traffic court was my Sunday school teacher. When I told him what had happened, he dismissed my ticket.

When I was 15, my mother married Hershel Honeycutt. They were married for about 25 years before my mother died in 1983. My stepfather had two sons, Charles and Robert. Robert went to live with his aunt when he was a young boy. Sadly, Charles became ill and died during his junior year in college.

That same year my father visited me. I hadn't seen him since I was five years old. While he was visiting with my mother, he let me drive his car around the block. When I hit the brakes, a bottle of liquor rolled out from under the seat. I poured the liquor into the street. I never saw my father again.

In the first and second grades I attended St. Joseph Catholic School. I was allowed to start school there when I was five. Otherwise, I would have had to wait another year to begin first grade because my birthday was in December. I remember that the priest and the nuns at St. Joseph were always nice and kind. Each day we worshiped together for about 30 minutes before class.

In the third grade I began attending Florence Elementary School. Because of my extracurricular jobs, I didn't have much time for school sports and other activities. During seventh and eighth grades I went to Appleby Junior High and played saxophone in the band. I was on the track team during my junior and senior years at Coffee High School and played football my senior year. I was active at First Baptist Church and participated in the Speaker's Tournament and the Bible Drill. I remember how exciting it was to go to the state tournament two different years.

I had other jobs in addition to my two year-round daily paper routes. At different times during high school, I worked at local restaurants and sold peanuts, popcorn, and Cokes at football games. Admittedly, my schoolwork suffered, but I'm convinced that the jobs I held as a young boy, teenager, and college student gave me a strong work ethic. That work ethic laid a good foundation for each of my four careers and taught me valuable life lessons about competition, people, and money management.

CHAPTER TWO

FIRST BAPTIST CHURCH
OF FLORENCE, ALABAMA

FROM THE TIME I was a child, I have always been drawn to church and to God's people. I have been a member of two churches: First Baptist Church in Florence, Alabama, and Bellevue Baptist Church in Memphis, Tennessee.

Being from a single parent home, God blessed me in many ways through my Sunday school teachers and pastors at First Baptist Church in Florence. They really loved God and they shared that love with me from the time I started attending church at the age of two or three. In fact, my mother told me that when I was about four, I decided to walk the few blocks to our church without letting her know. I was recuperating at home from the measles and I showed up at church in my pajamas!

I spent a lot of my growing up years at church learning about God's goodness through Vacation Bible School, Royal Ambassadors (RAs), Bible Drill, and other programs. I am so grateful for the godly men and women who invested their time in the boys and girls of our community.

Molding my character probably wasn't easy, because the people at church described me as "mischievous." Maybe I earned that label when a friend and I got into a little trouble with some firecrackers at church. Next to my photo in the high school yearbook was this phrase: "If mischief gets one to heaven, I'm well on my way." While that statement was meant to be humorous, I'm thankful that during this time my church family was teaching me what the Bible says about life's most important issue: how to get to heaven through a relationship with Jesus Christ.

Now, when I see the men and women at my church teaching our youth, I tell them how much I appreciate what they're doing. I share with them how godly men helped me when I was growing up without a father. The men of First Baptist Church were father figures to me. I'm thankful for everyone who teaches and encourages young boys and girls! They may not realize the impact they are having, but it is a great ministry. I don't know what might have happened to me without the support of my church family.

Another blessing from attending church was meeting my wife Beth. She and her family were good influences on me. I respected her dad, George Anderson Smith. He was an electrical engineer for the Tennessee Valley Authority (TVA). He taught me things that I hadn't learned, such as how to fish and hunt. He taught me how to change the oil in my car and how to cut wood with a chainsaw. He was a great example of a good husband and father.

Beth's parents provided a normal American family life for Beth and her two sisters, Joan and Donna. They enjoyed family vacations and the ordinary aspects of family life that were unknown to me. Proverbs 18:22 says, "He who finds a good wife finds a good thing and obtains favor from the Lord." Beth is my best friend.

A lot of young people stop attending church during their college years. I was blessed by the people in my life who made sure that I stayed involved in church ministries and activities while I was in college. I became a deacon when I was 23, and had opportunities to serve at First Baptist Church, including as a Sunday school teacher, RA leader, Sunday school director, deacon, chairman of the deacons, church treasurer, a member of the finance committee, and on two pastor search committees.

I also served on the "Together We Build" committee to make improvements to the church. In 1963, I watched as the steeple was installed on the new sanctuary. Beth and I were married on June 1, 1963, in the old First Baptist sanctuary just before the new one was completed. We have a mantel at home made from wood that came from the old sanctuary. It was a great feeling to see all our plans and work become reality.

Through the years we had a number of pastors at First Baptist Church and I loved them all. It seemed like every two or three years we got a new minister. I felt sad to see each one leave, but when the next minister came, I liked him even better than the one before. I remember Rev. Pete Woodruff, Rev. Hudson Baggett, Rev. John DeForre, Rev. Otis Brooks, Rev. W.C. Garland, and Rev. Sid Sample. I was on the pulpit committees when Rev. Garland and Rev. Sample were called to be our pastors.

Being in church has always been a special worship experience for me. I believe that God had a plan for me, and I was sensitive to it. I know that God's desire is to have all His people in church, but some of us don't respond to it. It's true that we can worship the Lord in different ways, but for me, the best way to worship is at church. Serving with people on various committees and in different roles also taught me about group dynamics, something that proved to be extremely important in my careers.

CHAPTER THREE

COLLEGE AND EARLY MARRIED YEARS

AFTER GRADUATING from high school, I enrolled at Florence State College, which is now The University of North Alabama. I didn't have much time for sports because of my paper routes, but I did play football my freshman year without a scholarship. After it became clear that I'd only be able to get a half-scholarship my sophomore year, I gave up the idea of playing football. I've never regretted that choice because I wouldn't have been a great athlete, and I could have had injuries that would have been with me for the rest of my life.

I'm glad I went to college in my hometown. Most of my friends went away to college, but many of them came back to Florence after a year or two. At Florence State there were no fraternities, so I didn't know I was missing anything. Actually, I believe I was better off because I gained experience and training through the work I did while going to school. I developed mental toughness and competence that helped prepare me for the tremendously difficult job I would have at Schilling Enterprises 20 years in the future.

It's interesting how God uses people we meet to help us with decisions. When I started college in 1960, I planned to become a lawyer. However, later I realized it would take seven years of college to achieve a law degree. I was working my way through school and decided that I needed to finish my college education and start a career. During my sophomore year, one of my newspaper customers, Dr. Roy Stevens, Dean of the Business Department at Florence State, suggested that I consider majoring in accounting. I'm glad I took his advice!

Although I was not always a strong student when it came to grades, I had good common sense which I successfully applied to various situations. I wanted to be a Certified Public Accountant (CPA). Two months before I graduated from Florence State College in the spring of 1964, I accepted a job offer from Huff & Compton, a CPA firm in Florence.

Beth and I had been married for nearly a year when I went to work as an accountant. We lived in a one-bedroom upstairs apartment in my mother's home when our daughter Leslie was born. We didn't acquire hospital insurance in time for it to cover Leslie's birth, but the doctor kindly gave us a student discount because we were both in college. Beth had to postpone her studies, but after two years she returned to college and graduated with a degree in elementary education. She later returned to school and earned a master's degree.

Two years later, we bought our first home for $13,900, paying a $600 down payment and a monthly payment of $85. Our first home was a prefabricated 990-square-foot house. Many great memories took place in that small space we called home.

CHAPTER FOUR

MY SECOND CAREER: PUBLIC ACCOUNTING

IN COLLEGE I MAJORED in accounting with a minor in economics. Although I wanted to be in public accounting, I didn't realize how hard it would be to get a job at a CPA firm in Florence, Alabama. I also didn't realize how low my starting salary would be.

As I prepared to graduate, I applied for jobs with local CPA firms. The two largest firms in Florence were Whitmon & Rutledge and Huff & Compton. Both firms employed about ten people, including the partners who were CPAs. I interviewed with these two firms during my senior year of college, but neither had an opening. I also interviewed with Byron Nicely, a single practitioner. Mr. Nicely's practice was growing and he needed help. So I got my first accounting job in January, 1964.

I still had my rural paper route for the *Birmingham News,* which Beth and I delivered seven days a week. Beth and her sister agreed to deliver the papers for me while I worked after school with Mr. Nicely. Beth was pregnant at the time, so this was a challenge for her!

After three months of working with Mr. Nicely, both accounting firms that I had originally interviewed with recruited me. While I will always be grateful to Mr. Nicely for giving me a starting job, I thought that I could gain more training and experience at a larger firm. In April of 1964, two months before graduation, I accepted a position with Huff & Compton, CPAs.

In 1964 the national average starting salary for accounting graduates was approximately $500 a month. In Florence, Alabama, the starting salary was one half of the national average. The starting salary was just a little more than Beth and I had been earning with our paper route. But I wanted to be in public accounting, so I accepted the job.

At that time in the state of Alabama, you had to work two years before you could take the CPA exam. It was a rigorous and comprehensive four-part test. I took review courses at the

University of Alabama and committed to spending many hours studying to prepare for this big challenge. I was fortunate enough to pass all parts of the exam except business law on my first attempt. I invested more time studying and passed business law on the next exam. To this day, I clearly recall the sense of excitement and accomplishment I felt when I received my CPA Certificate in May, 1967.

At that time I was making about $600 a month, and I thought that things would change immediately. I expected Huff & Compton to make me a partner and increase my salary substantially. While that did not happen, a few months after I received my CPA Certificate, one of our clients offered me the position of Chief Financial Officer at his company. Although it was a relatively small company, the position gave me the opportunity to learn how to handle financial operational responsibility and authority. I thought that gaining this perspective would make me a better professional. I was correct. The CFO's job was challenging, and I learned the lessons of day-to-day operations. However, I realized that my passion was for public accounting. I missed the diversity of projects, the different clients, and the professional development opportunities of public accounting.

Fortunately, Huff & Compton wanted me to return to their company. In fact, they made me a partner and I remained at Huff, Compton & Smith until January, 1980, when we moved to Memphis.

During my 16 years with Huff, Compton & Smith, I had opportunities to learn about a wide range of businesses. Mr. Huff and Mr. Compton were former Internal Revenue Service agents. They generously helped me research tax law questions. I had a real passion for public accounting. My favorite areas were income tax and estate planning.

As I worked with a broad range of clients, I observed their operating styles. I learned about a variety of businesses as I helped our clients buy, sell, and expand their businesses. I worked with accountants, lawyers, bankers, insurance agents, and business owners in construction, newspapers, motels, restaurants, medical, and other industries. I also had opportunities to travel all over the country.

One of our clients was WOWL, a TV and radio broadcasting station in Florence. They gave me a press-pass which I sometimes used when my family and I attended ballgames. It enabled us to go onto the field at the 1979 Sugar Bowl when the University of Alabama defeated Penn State University for the National Collegiate Football Championship. At that football game, Leslie and Beth's sister were able to get Coach Paul "Bear" Bryant's autograph.

Another client was a real estate developer/ investor. Although he didn't have a high school education, he was very successful at building homes and apartments and buying hotels. As his accountant, I went with him one cold day to meet with bankers at a bank in Boston when he was buying two hotels in Alabama. It was educational to watch my client, a master negotiator, at work. The bankers, most with MBAs, greatly underestimated my client, and he cleverly closed the deal without ever offering a price!

Because I was genuinely interested in different facets of public accounting, I learned a great deal about people and the business world. As a young man starting out, I focused more on developing professionally than on making money. That solid business background pre-pared me for my third career at Schilling Enterprises.

CHAPTER FIVE

MY THIRD CAREER: SCHILLING ENTERPRISES

MOST BUSINESS OWNERS and managers would agree that a strong work ethic is necessary to be a good leader. There are exceptions, but overall, most successful leaders set good examples by working hard. The work ethic I developed from my paper routes and other jobs while in school, plus the diversity of my experiences as a CPA, gave me mental strength and experience to help me begin my third career.

My career at Schilling Enterprises began in January, 1980. At that time the company owned and operated ten different businesses. The operations ranged from automobiles to HVAC.

Neal Schilling founded the company that grew into Schilling Enterprises. In 1929, while working for the Ford Motor Company plant in

Memphis, Tennessee, Mr. Schilling saw a business opportunity that developed into his first company. He established Dealers Transport Company that quickly and efficiently moved the newly manufactured Ford automobiles to Ford dealer showrooms.

In the early days of his transportation company, Mr. Schilling worked at the Ford plant during the day, drove the Ford cars to Arkansas dealerships at night, and rode the bus back to Memphis in time to get to work the next day. As his delivery operation grew, he hired college students to deliver cars for him and later devised a flatbed truck for hauling cars. His innovation in car transporting made him one of the pioneers in today's car and truck hauling business.

Mr. Schilling continued to acquire businesses in the Mid-South until he died in 1970. In addition to Dealers Transport Company, Schilling Enterprises owned and operated a Ford Tractor Distributorship, Mills Morris Auto Parts, with two large warehouses and eight retail stores located in Memphis and in Jackson, Mississippi, the York Heating and Air-Conditioning distributorship for the state of Alabama, Dealers Industrial Power Company, a distributor for Ford engines and irrigation pumps, and finally, Lincoln-Mercury automobile dealerships located in Alabama and Tennessee.

In the 1940s and 1950s, Schilling purchased 448 acres in Collierville, Tennessee, to use for his Ford tractor distributorship. He would bring his dealers there to compare the Ford tractors with other brands of tractors. When Ford Motor Company bought the distributorship from Mr. Schilling, he raised cattle on the property. In 1980, Ford Motor Company leased the land for ten years and used it just as Schilling had in earlier years.

My association with Schilling began in an unusual way. In 1973, as a partner at Huff, Compton & Smith CPAs, the owner of a failed automobile dealership retained me to assist in closing his business. This gentleman later became the general manager of Schilling's Gateway Lincoln-Mercury dealership in Sheffield, Alabama, and he introduced me to the president of Schilling Enterprises. Through this seemingly routine accounting project, I was introduced to the company where I would spend the majority of my working life! You never know how or when God will open doors.

When Mr. Schilling died in 1970, his long-time accountant became president of the companies. Although Mr. Schilling had advised his wife to sell the companies after he died, she chose to keep them.

The new president decided to employ outside accountants for each of the business operations. The general manager of the Schilling Lincoln-Mercury dealership in Sheffield, Alabama, (the gentleman I had helped earlier) suggested that Schilling use Huff, Compton & Smith. After this introduction I gradually began to handle different work assignments for the president. One was closing down a Ford dealership in Decatur, Alabama. Another was helping with a theft problem at one of the Memphis dealerships. Over a seven-year period, I began working with all the companies.

In the late 1970s, Schilling Enterprises embarked on two capital projects that required significant financing. The capital projects involved new facilities construction and new equipment for Dealers Transport Company and new facilities construction at one of the Memphis Lincoln-Mercury dealerships. These were large capital projects that required loans of several million dollars. The projects and loan arrangements took place at a most difficult time in the U.S. economy. The loans were structured as short-term notes to be refinanced with long-term debt. In 1979, the economy was bad and getting worse; interest rates climbed as high as 20% in early 1980. The tremendous increase in interest rates greatly increased the expense of financing the projects with long-term debt.

Added to the impact of a bad economy and high borrowing cost was bad news from Ford Motor Company regarding the termination of our contract to deliver new Ford cars and trucks. This devastating news was, of course, delivered after we had invested in the Dealers Transport facilities and equipment capital project.

On a cold day in January, 1980, I got a call from representatives of First Tennessee Bank in Memphis. They were concerned about the future of the company and had talked to Mrs. Schilling and Schilling's president about the need for additional management. The First Tennessee Bank representatives proposed the possibility of my coming to work at Schilling. I decided that it would be worthwhile to travel to Memphis to discuss the company's management needs and if my training and business experience could be of service. After the meeting with Mrs. Schilling and Schilling's president, I met with the First Tennessee Bank representatives for several hours. These meetings resulted in the retirement of Schilling's president and my appointment as president of Schilling Enterprises.

The plan was for me to spend several days a week in Memphis and return to Florence on the weekends to continue my work with Huff, Compton & Smith. Looking back on it, I believe that was God's way of easing me into the job. If I had had to commit to moving to Memphis immediately, I doubt that I would have accepted the offer.

I quickly realized that traveling back and forth to Memphis would not work long-term. I was working Monday through Thursday in Memphis and Friday through Sunday in Florence. When I went home to Florence, my partners and clients wanted to know when I was going to finish my work in Memphis and come home permanently. At the same time, people in Memphis wanted to know when I was going to move my family to Memphis.

After a couple of months of living in two places, I told Beth that I wasn't going to be able to continue this schedule. My career was in charge of my life and that was clearly not the way I wanted to live. When we married, Beth said she would go anywhere with me. But after 16 years in Florence, she wasn't excited about moving to Memphis. Neither was our 15-year-old daughter Leslie. Nevertheless, in March, 1980, after talking with my family and with Mrs. Schilling, our family decided that I would sell my interest in the accounting practice in Florence and move to Memphis. Sometimes we face risks that could have tremendous effects on our families and careers. If we feel God's leading, we need to be willing to step out and take the challenge.

Mrs. Schilling's attorneys prepared an agreement for me to purchase half of the company stock from her. Later this agreement was amended for me to purchase the remaining fifty percent.

When I took over as president of Schilling Enterprises the companies were struggling financially. We owed the Internal Revenue Service almost a million dollars in back payroll taxes and millions to the banks in Memphis and Ford Motor Credit Corporation. The transport company's losses were huge.

In late April of 1980, an executive of Ford Motor Company's traffic division called and asked me to come to Detroit the next day—and to come alone. At the meeting we exchanged pleasantries and then he dropped the bomb on me. I was informed that Ford was going to terminate our Dealers Transport business over the next five weeks. This was a relationship that had existed for 50 years.

This news was a real blow to Schilling Enterprises. Dealers Transport Company was the first company that Mr. Schilling started in 1929. It was a large operation with personnel, equipment, and terminals in Louisville and Lyndon, Kentucky; Memphis, Tennessee; Baton Rouge and New Orleans, Louisiana; and Jackson, Mississippi. After stating their intentions, the Ford executives told me that they knew that I could hire attorneys and fight their decision, but they assured me that their decision was final.

In 1980, all transport trucking companies were struggling because of the bad economy. Ford Motor Company's plan was to consolidate their business to a small group of car haulers and give these haulers all their business. After the 50-year relationship with Schilling, I was totally surprised by their decision to terminate us first. Perhaps they reasoned that as the company's new president I would just accept our fate without challenging the mega corporation's decision.

I returned to Memphis on Thursday and informed our attorneys and bankers of the situation. With everything at stake, they strongly suggested that I go back to Detroit and try to get the decision reversed. I traveled to Dearborn, Michigan, on Sunday and checked into a hotel that faced the Glass House, Ford Motor Company's world headquarters.

Monday morning I went to Ford's traffic division and asked them to reconsider, but they declined. Next, I met with the Ford executive in charge of the traffic division. He also declined to reconsider the decision to terminate our relationship. From there, I went through several more layers of Ford's executive hierarchy until I was allowed to meet with Harold Poling, the executive vice president. He and the other Ford executives at that meeting were courteous, but they upheld the decision to take away our business over the next five weeks. After two full days meeting with anyone and everyone at Ford, it appeared that I was running out of decision makers to try to persuade that they were making a mistake.

On Wednesday afternoon, alone in my hotel room, I reached a really low point. It was at this low point that one of the defining moments of my life occurred. As I looked out my hotel window at Ford's formidable Glass House, I knew that I lacked the resources to deliver myself and my company. I was at a dead end. And that's when the turning point occurred.

I will never forget what happened next. My hotel room telephone rang. It was an unexpected call from the manager of the Ford Motor Credit office in Memphis, a man I had met for the first time only a few days earlier. As he spoke, his words were like the five smooth stones that David used to slay Goliath: "We are praying for you." It encouraged me immensely and reminded me that Ford might be a giant compared to Harry Smith, but they are nothing compared to the God who was about to deliver me. I believe that God prompted this man to call and encourage me at precisely the time I needed it most. Knowing that people were praying for me strengthened me for the battles we had to fight to keep our business.

We put Dealers Transport Company into Chapter Eleven bankruptcy/reorganization protection and filed a lawsuit against Ford Motor Company for illegally terminating an implied contract that had existed for 50 years. While this litigation was in progress, we continued to operate three Lincoln-Mercury dealerships and a Ford Industrial Engine distributorship. So on one hand, we had filed a lawsuit against Ford Motor Company, while on the other hand, we were still doing business with them as well as with Ford Motor Credit.

I learned a whole new vocabulary while working with the bankruptcy attorneys. For example, in meetings they used terms like "down the tube" and "belly-up." This was very alarming when I heard those words used in reference to our company!

Another high stress point occurred on December 31, 1980, the last day of a very difficult year. One of the banks that we had borrowed from threatened to force us into Chapter 7 liquidation if they were not paid in full within 30 days. Being forced into Chapter 7 Bankruptcy would have resulted in us closing the companies and selling our assets. After this meeting I was distraught, and I walked out into the alley to collect myself. I needed someone or something to encourage me not to give up. And I got what I needed! My next appointment that day was with one of our attorneys. After I related the bank's threat of Chapter 7, he calmly assured me that he believed everything was going to be okay. Again God gave someone the encouraging words I needed to hear at just the right time.

As stressful as this all was, we did experience some high points along the way. In May of 1980 we closed our last Dealers Transport location, the truck loading and unloading dock in Lyndon, Kentucky. This facility was built adjacent to Ford Motor Company's only large truck manufacturing location. Historically, the Lyndon facility had been used by Ford's Truck Division to mount their new trucks before turning them over to Dealers Transport for delivery to the Ford Truck Dealer locations. We decided that if Ford was going to take our business away from us, we would control the timetable in order to maintain some bargaining power.

There were about 20 attorneys and bankers in my office when I made the telephone call to the truck plant manager in Lyndon, Kentucky.

He had run up two flights of stairs and was out of breath when he answered the call. I had him on the speaker phone and told him that afternoon we were closing our Lyndon loading and unloading truck facility. His response was, "You can't do that." And I said, "Well, I've got about 15 lawyers in the room with me who say that we *can* do it and we're doing it today at 4:00 p.m." There was a long pause on the other end of the telephone.

We did exactly what we said we were going to do, and it gave us the leverage we needed. Since Ford could no longer use our facility, they had to park trucks all over the yard. When winter came, they were still working outside in the rain, snow, and ice, mounting the trucks for delivery. This situation provided us with the negotiating clout we needed to help settle our lawsuit. Ford had underestimated our ability to defend our rights.

We took our $50 million, triple-damages lawsuit to court. The lawsuit was filed on May 13, 1980, which, coincidentally, was Mrs. Schilling's birthday. It was the largest bankruptcy case that had ever been filed in Memphis. We informed bankruptcy judge, William Leffler, that we wanted a trial by jury.

He chuckled a little and commented that he had never had a bankruptcy case tried by a jury in his court. Judge Leffler was a most impressive man. In his courtroom the rights of our small company were as important as the rights of any giant corporation. He was always firm but courteous in his courtroom. When the lawsuit was over I wanted to thank him, but he died before the case was fully settled. I did tell his family how grateful I was for his fairness and even-handedness. I attended his funeral and quietly whispered, "Judge Leffler, thank you."

Other divisions of Ford Motor Company were sympathetic with us for what the traffic division had done. We were dealing with the sales division of Lincoln-Mercury, Ford Motor Credit Corporation, the parts and service division of Ford Motor Company, the industrial engine division, and other related divisions. The three men in the traffic division who were responsible for the decision to terminate our business were all placed in different jobs or left Ford Motor Company. However, at this point Ford Motor Company's management team obviously felt they had no other recourse than to support the position these men had taken and to continue with the lawsuit.

The Dealers Transport trucks were relocated and parked at Schilling Farms (448 acres of land we owned in Collierville, a suburb of Memphis). There were more than a hundred trucks parked row after row. One cold winter day we had to etch Vehicle Information Numbers with pencil and paper so that we could obtain titles for the trucks whose titles had been lost and were in the process of being sold.

Another interesting thing that happened during this time involved a huge computer system that had just been installed at Dealers Transport Trucking Company. For over a year, a national computer company had been writing a software program that would track the cars' and trucks' location from the time they left the terminal until they arrived at the dealership. The computer company had invested hundreds of thousands of dollars in this software program which had just been completed.

We were leasing the software program and the computer hardware for $42,000 a month when Dealers Transport filed for bankruptcy protection. We paid the current monthly invoice of $42,000, and the computer company miraculously accepted it. They picked up the hardware equipment in full payment of any claims that they might have on Dealers Transport for future lease payments.

Ford worked with us to negotiate a settlement. Ford Motor Company had legal counsel in Memphis, as did Ford Motor Credit. Our attorneys worked with their attorneys to negotiate a settlement that would lower our bank loans to an amount we could repay. These negotiations went on for several months. In February of 1981, settlement agreements were reached with Ford Motor Company, Ford Motor Credit Corporation, and the various banks. Ford made many financial concessions and guaranteed loans on assets purchased from us to get our business back on track.

We paid our creditors 100 cents on the dollar, which is unusual in bankruptcy court. Both Mrs. Schilling and I wanted to pay our creditors all that was owed them. She always said, "Do what's right and everything will be okay."

A lot of great things came out of that difficult time when we were fighting to save our businesses. I had come from a three-partner accounting firm to assume the presidency of Schilling Enterprises with less than optimal background and business experience. I was 37 years old when I took the job at Schilling, and the challenge was overwhelming. I was in far over my head, but God sent people to help me. After we concluded the lawsuit and got our businesses re-focused on their objectives, associates would say, "Harry, you did a great job of working all that out." It was embarrassing to me because there was no doubt that it was God and not me. I give Him all the glory and praise for seeing me through it.

During those months of negotiations and major changes, I learned a lot about the importance of relationships. I met attorneys, bankers, accountants and other professionals representing the different companies and we got along well. Today, 30 years later, I'm still friends with attorneys that represented the other side. We have laughed about it and even joked about having a party with some of us wearing white hats and others wearing black hats. I learned that it is important not to isolate yourself from people who see things differently or take an alternative position. Maintaining good relationships has been critical to my effectiveness as a corporate leader.

A positive aspect of becoming president at that crucial time was the fact that I was not part of the problem that had caused the financial disaster. Therefore, I had the luxury of an unbiased point of view. My job was to solve problems and take the responsibility of getting the business back on track. I was already familiar with each of the companies because I had worked with them as their outside accountant. I knew the people and the problems at each company. Starting with this clean slate made taking the actions required to solve the problems clearer, even though they were still difficult.

Looking back, I can see how God prepared me every step of the way. Delivering newspapers prepared me. Being in church prepared me, and working at the accounting firm prepared me. I also learned more about the power of prayer. Beth, my friends, and I prayed for wisdom and guidance. God answered our prayers. It was a very hard time, but He was always there.

When the bankruptcy settlement was reached in February of 1981, several Schilling companies had been sold or closed. We were ready to grow again. At this point our annual revenues were approximately $50 million and we employed about 300 associates. From the original group of companies, the York HV/AC distributorship, Dealers Industrial Power Company, and our automobile dealerships remained. We decided to shift our focus from a broadly diversified group of companies to a concentrated focus on our automobile dealerships. As the right opportunities presented themselves, we sold the York operation and the Industrial Power operation. We stuck with our business plan and were up to our necks in the automobile business!

The automobile dealership business was fast moving for us. We profitably bought and sold, opened and closed automobile dealerships throughout the South for nearly 25 years. Here is a brief history of our exciting dealership businesses that started with the Lincoln-Mercury dealerships.

We purchased a Porsche-Audi franchise and moved it to Union Avenue with the Lincoln-Mercury dealership. We purchased a Saab and Maserati franchise which we later sold along with the Porsche and Audi franchises. We opened a Chevrolet dealership in downtown Memphis and closed it about 18 months later. In 1985, we purchased a Lincoln-Mercury dealership in Little Rock, Arkansas, and sold it in 1996. In 1987, we opened a third Memphis Lincoln-Mercury dealership on Covington Pike and re-branded all the dealerships to Schilling Lincoln-Mercury.

In 1989, we purchased a Jeep franchise from the Chrysler Corporation and moved it adjacent to the Lincoln-Mercury dealership on Mendenhall in Memphis. It turned out to be the most profitable of all our dealerships, and it came about because of my relationship with the manager of the Ford Motor Credit Company I met during the Schilling financial crisis. The man who had called to encourage me in my hotel room across from the Glass House was the one who told me about this business opportunity.

In 1996, we sold the dealership on Covington Pike to Ford Motor Company and purchased a Toyota dealership on the corner of Millbranch and Brooks Road in Memphis. We sold that dealership a couple of years later. In 1997, the dealership on Union Avenue was combined with the Mendenhall dealership, leaving Schilling with one Lincoln-Mercury dealership in Memphis.

As of 1999, Schilling owned the Lincoln-Mercury dealership on Mendenhall and the Jeep dealership. Negotiations were successful to buy the Chrysler dealership on Mt. Moriah Road in Memphis and to combine the Jeep and Chrysler dealerships. This occurred in 2000 as part of Chrysler's Project 2000. In 2003, we purchased a Dodge franchise and combined it with our Jeep and Chrysler dealership. We sold this dealership in 2003. We sold our last dealership, the Lincoln-Mercury dealership on Mendenhall, in 2005. I believe God allowed us to sell and receive good prices for our automobile dealerships before the downturn in the economy.

As you can see from our history, we were very busy in the automobile business. Looking back, it was exciting and we took the opportunity to build long lasting business relationships and friendships. There were times Beth and I were with the Ford Motor Company executives at social events. These events included the Lincoln-Mercury New Car Introduction Shows, the National Automobile Dealers annual meetings, and the Lincoln-Mercury National Dealer Council meeting.

I was elected to serve two terms on the Lincoln-Mercury National Dealer Council meetings by the dealers in my district. There were about 20 dealers from across the country on the Dealer Council who served for two years.

During these meetings, select dealers were invited to sit at tables with top Ford executives. There was a pecking order as to where they sat. The chairman of Ford Motor Company sat at table #1, the president at table #2, and so on down the line. Because we had five Lincoln-Mercury dealerships, several times we were invited to sit at table #1 with the chairman.

On one of those occasions, Beth and I were at Chairman Don Peterson's table. Beth was seated next to him, and one of her questions was, "How many employees does your company have?" His answer was, "350,000." Beth replied, "Harry has 350!"

The Lincoln-Mercury National Council met for four days twice a year in Detroit. On the last day of one of those meetings, we had lunch at the Glass House on the twelfth floor with Ford Motor Company's chairman and his executive team. I would never have imagined in April, 1980, when I was in that hotel room in despair, that a few years later I would be having lunch with Ford Motor Company's chairman.

In 1990, I purchased the other half of Mrs. Schilling's stock. The following year we began developing Schilling Farms, the 448-acre property in Collierville, along with my partner, Boyle Investment Company. My vision was for Schilling Farms to be a place where families could live, work, play, and worship. I wanted to include in the deed that alcohol would not be sold or served at any business that was established on the property. My reasoning was that if Schilling Farms belongs to God—and it does—what would He say about that? Thankfully, my business partners were agreeable to that restriction. They have been great partners for almost 20 years, and Schilling Farms has had great success.

In 2003, a church friend of mine, Steve Tucker, and I purchased Circle Y Saddle Company in Yoakum, Texas. The company was experiencing financial difficulties and was being managed by a consultant hired by The Bank of New York until a sale could be made. Steve and I traveled to New York City and negotiated a deal to purchase the company. It was the largest saddle manufacturer in the United States and a good business venture for us. This experience allowed me to learn more about manufacturing.

Fortunately, after a couple of years, the company became profitable. Steve was a great partner. I sold my stock to him in 2009.

CHAPTER SIX

MANAGING A BUSINESS

MANAGING A BUSINESS is not easy. You must be a leader and a manager and there's a difference between the two. A leader knows what's best to do and a manager knows the best way to do it. Leaders help set the vision and motivate others to achieve the company's goals. Managers organize and structure the company's activities to achieve the goals.

Prior to joining Schilling in 1980, I had little experience leading or managing a large number of employees. I had taken business management courses in college, but that had been 16 years earlier. Suddenly, I was the president of a group of companies with 1,000 employees and $100 million in annual revenues. To say that I was in over my head is an understatement!

As I mentioned in Chapter 4, my first year as president of Schilling was spent working through an intense economic situation made worse by a large debt burden. Our next challenge was to restructure the company in order to become financially sound and return to a growth cycle. In 1980 an attorney made a statement to me that stuck in my mind. He said, "It's one challenge to turn a company around; it's another challenge to run it." I quickly came to understand what he meant! If we were going to turn the companies around from financial disaster to operating successful businesses, I had to begin making difficult decisions such as which businesses we would keep, how many employees we would need, and other crucial decisions. I restructured the company and built a management team that shared my vision, value system, and philosophy.

My initial leadership and management skills came mostly by doing what seemed natural. Slowly, our company began to implement systems that helped us become more efficient. One of our biggest steps was preparing our company mission statement. Over a 12-month period I met with our entire workforce—from mechanics to managers—to develop a company mission statement. I wanted us all to work toward a set of business practices that were accepted and supported by the entire company. I wanted to create a culture of integrity for all at Schilling Enterprises. My desire was for our mission statement to represent the company's goals as stated by our employees and not merely my own.

After months of collaborating, we developed the following mission statement for our companies. I referred our employees to these guiding principles when they had a question about how to treat our customers or fellow employees. When we interviewed prospective employees, we explained our company's principles. We told them that if they didn't feel good about these principles they probably wouldn't enjoy working with us. These principles represented what our company stood for.

Schilling Guiding Principles

1. Practice honesty, integrity, and fairness in everything we do.
2. Assure every customer receives value, quality, and satisfaction.
3. Create an environment in which our employees can succeed.
4. Return to the community a share of the success we experience.
5. Consistently promote these Christian principles through our behavior.

Our value system led us to do some things differently than our competitors. In 1980 it was unusual for car dealership to be closed on Sundays, but we were. That change was made because I wanted our employees and their families to be able to worship together and have family time on Sundays. Consequently, we were able to attract men and women with strong family values to join our team. This caliber of employee made our team stronger. Truett Cathy, Chick-Fil-A's founder, has been a great role model for Christian businessmen to follow. From 1946, when he opened his first store, he had a policy of closing on Sundays. His reasons were both practical and spiritual. He wanted his employees to have the opportunity to rest and to worship if they chose to. This is part of his "recipe for success."

I also instituted a policy that no alcohol would be consumed on our property or served at company parties and picnics. These policies represented our commitment to "walk the walk" and not just "talk the talk." In our opinion, doing things differently from the norm had no negative impact upon our company or its business.

Another way our company promoted family values was by sponsoring a series of 30-second television message spots that aired locally. The purpose of the spots was not to make a sale; in fact, automobiles were not even mentioned. The purpose was to offer encouragement to people who needed a message of hope. We worked with a creative production team that understood our vision and helped us produce several of these inspirational spots. At the end of the television message, the name Schilling was mentioned as a sponsor. The over-whelmingly positive response from the community was rewarding to us all.

I would like to stress the importance of a value system in business (or in one's personal life). I believe that businesses tend to take on the values and personalities of their leaders and managers. If a company's leaders have core values of honesty, integrity, dignity, humility, courage, and fairness, there is a high probability that the company will manifest these qualities as it provides customer care and alignment of interest with its customers. These businesses have long life cycles because they promote trust and loyalty among their customers. Further-more, the right value system also promotes trust and loyalty among employees. Employees take ownership and want to be involved in a business that operates on Mrs. Schilling's advice: "Do what is right and everything will be okay."

CHAPTER SEVEN

MY FOURTH CAREER: NOT-FOR-PROFIT BOARD SERVICE

I CONSIDER MY FOURTH career to be my work with not-for-profit organizations. When my son-in-law, Rex Jones, took over the day-to-day operational leadership of Schilling Enterprises, this gave me the opportunity to spend a greater portion of my time working with not-for-profit organizations. I'm thankful to have had the opportunity to serve on the boards of a number of non-profit organizations. The life-changing work of these organizations cannot be overstated. Not-for-profit organizations need the same level of leadership, vision, and management expertise that any company requires.

Serving on these boards allows me to use my many years of business experience to help the organizations accomplish their goals. I dis-

covered that most organizations need leadership
as much as they need financial help. With the
right leadership, an organization can execute its
mission successfully. In turn, success attracts a
larger donor base to help them achieve their
purposes.

Serving on various boards has been a way for
me to give back to the community, something
that has been important to me in my personal,
as well as my business life. One of the points of
Schilling's mission statement was: "Return to
the community a share of the success we
experience." By being involved in community
service, I've had the opportunity to meet a wide
cross-section of people, and I've enjoyed the
camaraderie of fellow board members. As a
member of boards of directors, I have learned a
great deal about the operations of health care
organizations, educational institutions, and
others. It's very satisfying and a joy to be a part
of an organization when it functions in a
positive way.

At times it can be a struggle for a board
member to find the balance between being too
involved and not involved enough. Governance
is a big issue. The IRS and other governmental
agencies are putting more responsibility on

board members to be informed on what is happening and to be vocal on important issues.

Many times board members are chosen because they are friends with management or other board members. History illustrates that these boards are often ineffective because the members lack expertise, are unwilling to ask the hard questions, and typically do not disagree with management. These boards miss the point of providing expertise and guidance that helps the management teams achieve or surpass the organization's goals. It can be a challenge, therefore, to be an effective board member and to also have unity with management and fellow board members.

I have served on two boards where I couldn't be effective. I resigned from one, and I was not asked to return by another organization after being off the board for a year, which was unusual for that organization. I have read a lot about how to be a good board member and about governance. It's a fine line to walk, but when done with integrity, it works very well.

I will share with you the boards I have served on or continue to serve on. My desire has been to serve on boards that help people change/improve their lives. These boards focus on health, education, food and shelter, physical rehabilitation, and financial assistance.

The YMCA Metro Board helps members improve their physical condition in a Christian atmosphere. Good physical conditioning strengthens you physically and mentally, giving you the endurance to do your job well. The Salvation Army and Memphis Union Mission Boards help people who need food or shelter. I had never understood the magnitude of homelessness until I served on these two boards. They also provide rehabilitation assistance for people who are addicted to alcohol and drugs. I believe in these organizations because they help people the way that Jesus helped people during His time on Earth.

The Urban Youth Initiative Board focuses on helping young inner-city boys. They facilitate a mentoring program staffed by men who serve as good role models and counsel boys using Christian principles. With single-parent homes prevalent in our society, this organization seeks to support single moms by bringing some balance into boys' lives.

I had a wonderful experience serving on the Regional Medical Center (The MED) Board for six and a half years. The MED provides medical care for the underprivileged in our community. I also served on the Baptist Hospital Board for nearly ten years.

Over the years I have come to appreciate more and more the importance of Christian education. I am serving, or have served on, the Union University/ Foundation Boards, the Baptist College of Health Sciences, and Evangelical Christian School boards. These educational institutions provide students with a Christian perspective and a solid education foundation that equips them to serve the world as nurses, educators, scientists, artists, engineers, hospital technicians, businessmen and businesswomen, counselors, social workers, and in other professions.

The University Of Memphis Board Of Visitors/ Foundation Board helps the Memphis community in many ways. For example, the University of Memphis employs a large number of our citizens. The board has worked alongside current president, Dr. Shirley Raines, and her predecessors to improve academic programs by hiring brilliant professors, increasing research, and attracting high-achieving students. It has been a blessing to serve with many of my fellow Memphians and University leaders on this board, as well as on the Executive Advisory Committee of the Fogelman College of Business and Economics.

At the university level, I also serve on the foundation board of my alma mater, the University of North Alabama. The University of North Alabama (or Florence State College as it was named when I was a student) provided the educational foundation that allowed me to achieve success in business. It is an honor to have been asked to serve the university that has meant so much to me.

I have had the honor of serving on several other boards, including Downline Ministries, Prayers at Work, Ministry to Men, Love Worth Finding, Mid-America Baptist Theological Seminary, and Partners for the Homeless. I have also served on the Bellevue Foundation board at my church and now serve on the Hope Christian Community Foundation board.

Our family foundation's mission statement emphasizes helping faith-based ministries in our community. Our board executes our mission by contributing to churches and other ministries. It is very exciting and a great blessing for me to see our entire family involved in "giving back" and, as a family, celebrate the joy that giving brings to us.

My board service on the Collierville, Tennessee, Chamber of Commerce gave me the opportunity to work with community leaders to attract businesses to Collierville. We worked with the mayor and board of alderman in making Collierville a more business-friendly town. During this same time I served on the Mayor's Advisory Council.

The most rewarding board experience I have had began on February 5, 2008, when I was serving as chairman of the board of trustees for Union University located in Jackson, Tennessee. An EF4 tornado with winds up to 200 miles per hour nearly leveled the campus. Miraculously, none of the approximately 1,800 students on campus were killed. Several students were injured, but all have recovered. The tornado caused $40 million worth of damage to 31 buildings, rendering 80 percent of the campus unlivable.

While rejoicing at God's protection of precious human lives, we faced an enormous challenge. Eighteen dormitories—with students inside—had been demolished by the storm. The next day I met with President David Dockery, and the following weeks were spent developing plans to rebuild the campus. I practically lived in Jackson for three weeks.

In addition to preserving the lives of the students, God moved in the hearts of people locally and across the nation to help Union University financially recover from this crisis. Incredibly, by the time the fall semester began seven months later, brand new dorms were opened. We watched a miracle occur! This was a result of great cooperation between the board, Dr. Dockery and his staff and faculty, students, construction companies, the City of Jackson and Madison County officials, and the generous financial support of donors, including various branches of the Southern Baptist Convention, churches, and universities in Tennessee and across the country. It's hard to imagine any board and its stakeholders working together more smoothly. This was definitely an example of God taking something bad and making something good from it.

My fourth career represents one of the best times of my life. It has both thrilled and inspired me to witness self-sacrifice and commitment to making this world a better place. I am thankful to have worked with so many fine people that are true stewards of God's gifts of time, talents, and treasure, and who have dedicated their lives to helping those in need. I plan to continue serving on boards as long as I can make a contribution.

CHAPTER EIGHT

WORSHIP:
THE COMMON THREAD

THROUGH ALL FOUR careers, I have worshiped God and looked to Him for help. I have God to thank for everything good that has happened in my life. As I have trusted Him, He has always been there for me. The four main aspects of worship for me are evangelism, prayer and quiet time, stewardship, and unity.

Evangelism

AS CHRISTIANS we should pray and read our Bibles daily, worship at church, fellowship with other Christians, and share the good news of Jesus Christ with others.

The Bible powerfully states our responsibility to share the good news in Matthew 28:19-20. Jesus gave His disciples the Great Commission when He said, "Go and make disciples of all nations, baptizing them in the name of the Father and of the Son and of the Holy Spirit, and teaching them to obey everything I have commanded you. And surely I am with you always, to the very end of the age."

For many years I thought I could share the good news of Jesus with others by living a good life and setting a good example. Deep in my heart, I knew that I needed to do more, but I lacked the training and self-confidence I needed to share the good news with people that I didn't know. A program at my church, Evangelism Explosion (EE), taught me what to say and how to help people invite Jesus into their hearts and to make Him Lord of their lives.

I completed my EE training more than 20 years ago, but I still rely on it. I'm thankful my son-in-law Rex encouraged me as we went through the course together. Since we completed EE, I have had the blessing of training several dozen fellow church members and friends in this program. Over the years I have seen God work as He used our EE teams to share His good news and welcome many people into His saving grace.

EE is a 14-week course. Each trainer has two trainees who learn an outline that includes Bible verses and illustrations. It's a wonderful way for Christians to share with others how to make the biggest decision they will ever make: to invite Jesus into their hearts and to follow Him the rest of their lives. Every semester at EE I learned to be a more effective witness for Christ. I have been blessed to see so many come to know Jesus as their Lord and Savior through EE.

Why is it so hard to share Jesus with others? I think it is because the devil doesn't want us to. I have very seldom had anyone be rude to me when I sincerely approached them about where they were in their spiritual life. If people know you care about them, I think they are much easier to approach. If we are being obedient to Jesus and following the Holy Spirit's leading, He will honor our obedience and bless our efforts.

As I get older, I have learned not to resist the Holy Spirit's leadership about sharing Christ with others. I still miss opportunities, but not as many as I missed in the past. People face many challenges and sometimes God leads us to help people in their time of need. It may be to pray with them or help them in other ways. We may not always see the fruit of our work, but regardless we must always plant the seeds and hope for the harvest. Our responsibility is to be obedient to His leading.

When I see someone receive Jesus as Lord and Savior, I often tell them that someone, perhaps their mother or a friend, has been praying for them. The Holy Spirit led us to them to share the gospel and, as they received Jesus, they received the gift of eternal life. I encourage that person to share what has happened to them with their family, friends, and others—that they opened the door to their heart and invited Jesus into their life. What a blessing it is to be a part of what God is doing in the lives of other people!

Being involved in Evangelism Explosion has helped me in many ways. My wife even says that I am a better husband as a result of EE.

Stewardship

GOD BLESSES us in many ways and He expects us to be good stewards. Stewardship is a matter of faith and trust. The keys to being a good steward are to have *faith* that God will direct you to do the right thing and to *trust* Him to provide all you need to do His will. Stewardship is about responding to God's call. We are stewards of the time we have, how we use the talents God has given us, and how we use finances to support God's work.

Many times money is the focus of stewardship discussions. If the thought of giving 10% of your income away seems impossible, I'd like to share my thoughts and experiences with you. I learned as a child that God requires a tithe (10% of income) from each of His children. During my first career delivering newspapers, I made about $200 a month and I gave $2 a week to my church. I committed to God that when I graduated from college I would start tithing. I didn't realize I would only be making $250 a month, be married, and have a new baby! But I made the commitment, and I am thankful I kept it.

After graduating I honored my pledge, and our family gave $6.70 a week to church. It taught me two things. First, I learned some-thing about myself. I learned that I had the faith to follow God's requirement to give a tithe. Secondly, I learned that whatever I gave back to God was repaid to me in blessings beyond anything I could have imagined. We never missed any of the money we gave back to God. Over the years I have spoken to other Christians who tithed, and they told me that they, too, were blessed for being faithful to God. In Luke 12:34, Jesus said, "For where your treasure is, there your heart will be also." Having faith and being obedient regarding finances has freed me to focus on other important parts of life.

When I was in my 20s, my pastor encouraged me to increase our giving from 10 percent to 11 percent—to 12 percent—to 13 percent—and then to 14 percent. We did, and never missed the money we gave to God. He doesn't need our money, but He allows us to give it and blesses us for being faithful and obedient.

When I was in my 30s, I was a partner at Huff, Compton & Smith. During that time I became part owner of a land development company in Florence, Alabama. I committed to give 50% of my share of the profits to God's work.

Then God called me to Memphis to a challenging job with a lot of opportunity. With God's help we turned the companies around, and since that time more than 30 years ago, Beth and I have given half of our income to our church, a foundation we started, and to other charitable organizations.

Jesus said, "It is more blessed to give than to receive." It's true that you cannot out-give God. What blessings my family and I have received because of our faithfulness to God! We didn't give to get, but we were blessed because we gave.

I know that everything we have belongs to God and that we are merely stewards of what He has placed under our control. The Bible says, "Unto whom much is given, much will be required." I take that responsibility very seriously. I pray that I will know how to best invest what He has placed under my control and that I will give to the right ministries. Wisdom in giving comes by listening to and watching the Holy Spirit work in our lives.

Prayer and Quiet Time

I BELIEVE God answers our prayers through reading His Word, praying, receiving godly counsel, and through circumstances. It's amazing how many times I forget to pray about needs in my life. It's also amazing the blessings I receive when I finally remember to stop and ask God for help. Prayer works! The Bible says that we should "pray without ceasing." I think that means to always be in an attitude of prayer and to recognize that God is always with us.

During my prayer time, I refer to several lists that include prayer needs for my family, my friends, and people from my church. I pray during my quiet time and also throughout my daily routine. I will be driving in my car and sometimes glance up to the sky and pray to God.

Philippians 4:6 is my favorite verse in the Bible. It says, "Do not be anxious about anything, but in every situation, by prayer and petition, with thanksgiving, present your requests to God."

When we moved to Memphis and began attending Bellevue, I was sitting in a worship service with my daughter Leslie on a Wednesday night. She was sixteen years old at the time. Our pastor was preaching on Philippians 4:6. Leslie leaned over to me and said, "That's my favorite Bible verse."

From that time, it became my favorite verse, too. I try to live by this paraphrase of Philippians 4:6: "Don't worry about anything, pray about everything, tell God your needs, and don't forget to thank Him for His answers."

I have learned from the example of others the importance of stopping during the day to pray with and for others. I'm thankful for Beth's prayers for me during the day. Knowing that she is praying for me strengthens me. I'm also thankful for my friends who pray for my family and me. I believe that the gift of prayer is the greatest gift anyone can give.

In Steven Covey's book, *Seven Habits of Highly Effective People,* the author asks this question: "What one thing could you do in your life that would have the biggest impact?" My answer to that question is to improve my quiet time with the Lord. I believe that having an effective quiet time every day is the biggest challenge a Christian faces. We know how important it is, but we still struggle to do it consistently. God speaks most clearly and we learn the most when silence fills our heart.

To grow spiritually, God wants us to spend time alone with Him each day, praying and reading His Word, the Bible. This quiet time alone with God is important because He wants us to have a personal relationship with His Son Jesus. We want to be closer to Jesus, but we often put off having our quiet time.

In my personal mission statement I have made it my #1 priority to try to become more like Jesus. I know that the way to do that is to spend time with Him each day, preferably first thing in the morning before beginning my day. Yet it's so easy for me to allow the morning TV news, the newspaper, meetings, or other things to distract me from having quiet time with Jesus. Every day I should strive to read from the book of Psalms for thanksgiving and the book of Proverbs for wisdom.

Although men are to be the spiritual leaders of their homes, most men have a hard time praying and studying the Bible with their wives. Maybe it's because wives know their husbands better than anyone else does. They know whether or not we're sincere. We husbands have to live our faith in front of our wives every day. Thankfully, I'm doing better, but I'm not where I need to be. Almost every morning Beth and I read from a devotional book and our Bible. We pray together in the morning and at night before we go to sleep.

God wants couples to pray together because it builds unity in the family. For one thing, it's hard to be mad at each other and pray together. My pastors have always said, "It's hard for God to bless you if you don't have a good relationship with your wife." Next to my relationship with God, my relationship with Beth is the most important of my life.

Unity at Church

I BELIEVE that God wants all of us to worship in church, but some of us don't respond to His will. I know we can worship in different ways, like being in nature or by ourselves or through a television broadcast, but for me, being in church with other believers has always been the way I worship the Lord best.

I have been a member of only two churches: First Baptist Church in Florence, Alabama, and Bellevue Baptist Church in Memphis, Tennessee. Although we visited several churches in Memphis when we moved from Florence in 1980, we felt more at home at Bellevue. When we joined Bellevue, Dr. Adrian Rogers was the senior pastor. We had heard from many people about his great Bible preaching. When we heard him from the pulpit, we knew that his reputation was well deserved. He was a great preacher and a model Christian. Dr. Rogers was an inspiration to me and my family.

During the 25 years he was my pastor, I had the blessing to learn so much under his leadership. He was a wonderful teacher and role model who always sought God's will. He had the gift of making people feel special. I watched him on several occasions single out the common person or pastor from a small church and spend time with them. It was things like this that caused him to earn the respect of everyone. He taught us as a church family to love and pray for each other. Another thing I hoped to have learned from him was how to finish well.

Today, under the leadership of Pastor Steve Gaines, there is always something exciting going on at Bellevue because the church offers so many different ways to serve God. In addition to great sermons at the worship services, there are Bible studies and other activities for every age group. Through Dr. Gaines' vision, Bellevue is reaching people locally in unprecedented ways through a ministry known as Bellevue Loves Memphis. The church's outreach program is literally worldwide. I truly believe that our best days are to come.

Our entire family has been active at Bellevue. Since joining Bellevue, I have had the privilege of serving in a number of leadership positions. I have served as chairman of the deacons, chairman of the finance committee, Bridge to the Future Committee, missions committee, and pastor search committee.

Unity in church is very important. God expects His church to be unified. I have been in church all of my life and I have found some of the nicest—and some of the meanest—people inside the church. Over the years I have learned that a few disgruntled people can make a big sound, when in reality they are few in number. I call them the loud minority. I have also learned that the nicest people are usually the quietest. I call them the quiet majority. The body of Christ is a wonderful thing when it functions as God intends and serves in harmony. On the other hand, it can be very unpleasant when it doesn't.

A while back several members of our church were unhappy. This group caused other members to be unhappy, too. Thankfully, that time has passed. Our pastor, staff, and members are again worshiping in unity as the body of Christ. Several members went to other churches and found places of leadership there. I can see now how God used an unpleasant situation to move people to other places of service. During that time, many of us allowed the devil to take away our joy even though we should never let that happen. I admit that I did, but once I realized what had happened, I was able to get my joy back.

Unity in Families and with Friends

MY DESIRE for Rex and Leslie has always been for them to be happy. At first Leslie resisted the idea of Rex being my business partner, but he and I have always gotten along very well. I appreciate the way Beth and Leslie have encouraged Rex and me to keep the lines of communication open. Our family is blessed because we respect and love each other and we share the same spiritual values. We all go to church together and live in the same neighborhood.

As my grandsons have become teenagers, I've had the privilege of taking each one on a trip, just the two of us. My oldest grandson Barrett and I went to the Holy Land when he was 15 years old. Our pastor, Dr. Adrian Rogers, connected us with his tour guide in Israel. We had him as our personal guide for a day and a half. The man refused to let us pay him for his services because of his respect and love for Dr. Rogers. From there we flew to Rome and then traveled by train to Florence and Venice, Italy. We then drove through Germany and Switzerland.

Harrison likes cars. When he was 17, I took him to the Bob Bondurant Driving School in Phoenix, Arizona. There he spent two days driving real race cars on the track. We attended an Arizona Diamondback baseball game and visited Sedona, Arizona, where Harrison rode a Jeep in the desert. We had a great time.

I took Walker, my youngest grandson, on a trip out west also. We visited the Grand Canyon, Lake Meade, and Hoover Dam. We also saw two Cirque du Soleil shows in Las Vegas. Walker enjoyed riding roller coasters and a dune buggy in the desert. I'll never forget the special times I've shared with my grandsons, and I think the boys will have good memories of our trips, too.

There is something special about the relationship between grandparents and grandchildren. In my office I have hung a framed copy of a poem that my oldest grandson wrote in honor of my fifty-fifth birthday.

Barrett was only seven years old when he wrote this:

"My Papa"

by Barrett A. Jones

He is true.
He is nice.
He is sincere.
He drinks Root Beer.

He is sweet.
He is kind.
He is thoughtful.
He has a good mind.

He is special.
He is good.
Sometimes he lets me ride on his hood.

He takes me to church and also to Perkins.
Sometimes we even see Mrs. Jerkins.

Today is his birthday. He's fifty-five.
I can't believe he's still alive.

But he is, and I'm glad.
'cause he's the best Papa a boy ever had!

I love you, Papa, you're the BEST!!!
I'll see you soon at Laser Quest!

CHAPTER NINE

GUIDANCE WHEN
MAKING DECISIONS

THERE WAS A TIME in my life when I was hesitant to pray for God's will because I was afraid that it wouldn't be what I wanted. However, I've learned from experience that God knows what I need better than I do. I realized that even when He didn't give me what I wanted, what He gave me was better than what I wanted. Now it's easier for me to pray for God's will when I'm trying to make a decision and I need guidance.

I believe that it is important to seek God's guidance at all times, but especially when you are faced with a big decision. For example, several years ago I considered running for mayor in the town of Collierville, Tennessee. Never before had I had political ambitions, and after thinking about it for a while, I dismissed the idea. But it wouldn't go away. It kept coming back into my mind, so I began to pray about it.

A couple of months later I asked Beth what she thought about me running for mayor. She didn't think it was a good idea, but she wasn't as negative about it as I'd thought she might be. I also talked with Leslie and Rex, and they thought that running for mayor was an interesting idea. I mentioned it to a few friends and community leaders in Collierville and asked them to pray about it with me.

I was concerned about whether God was leading me to run for mayor or if it was just something I wanted to do. I was also concerned that running for mayor might affect three specific areas of my life: my character and reputation, my family, and my health.

While on a vacation trip with Beth, we discussed again the idea of me running for mayor. With some hesitancy, she agreed to support me. I talked with some friends again, and I counseled with my pastor and asked him to pray for me about my decision. A good friend advised me to find out what Beth *really* thought—not what she thought *I* wanted to do. I followed his advice, and Beth assured me that she would support me if I chose to run for mayor. This was on a Tuesday; I needed to make a decision by Thursday.

About 3:00 on Wednesday morning, I woke up and couldn't go back to sleep. I went downstairs to have a snack and to look over my prayer list. Instead I picked up my Bible to read in the book of Proverbs. While turning the pages to Proverbs, I paused momentarily and noticed that my Bible was opened to the Old Testament book of Job. The subheadings in the first part of Job caught my eye. While these subheadings were written by man and not by God, I believe God had an important message for me. The three subheadings related directly to my three specific concerns about running for mayor. The first subheading was "Satan attacks Job's character." The second was "Job loses his property and children." The third subheading was "Satan attacks Job's health." These were the exact three things that had concerned me.

Later that morning, I turned to the chapter in Psalms that I had intended to read the night before. In my Living Bible I read Psalm 16:7: "I will bless the Lord who counsels me. He gives me wisdom in the night." To me, this was a direct confirmation of what I had read in Job in the early hours of the morning. God had counseled me in the night! Then I read Proverbs 16:1 which says, "We can always prove that we are right, but is the Lord convinced?" Proverbs 16:3 went on to say, "Commit your work to the Lord; then it will succeed." Then the last verse of that chapter says, "We toss the coin, but it is the Lord who controls its decision."

I realized that I had made my plans, but the final outcome was in God's hands. You can ask 100 or 200 people what they think about something, but if God tells you something different, then it really doesn't matter. His answer is the one that counts. Obviously, I dropped the idea of running for mayor and looking back, I can see it was the right decision.

When I am making decisions, I pray and ask God to work them out in the way He thinks best. That's because in my human limitations I don't know what's best. I believe that having the desire to do what God wants is the first step in making the right decisions. Then He will lead you, often by opening or closing "doors."

CHAPTER TEN

MY NINE LIFE PRINCIPLES

Life Principle #1

Be interested in everything you do.

DO YOU HAVE a passion for your work? Can you find something interesting about every person you meet and about every job you do? How can you achieve balance in all areas of your life while working passionately on your career?

These are important questions. I recommend that you find a job you like and build a good professional foundation. When beginning your career, don't focus on the monetary aspect; that will come if you focus on developing skills and adding value to your assignments.

My first job after college paid a starting salary that was about half the national average for accounting graduates. But I had a passion for public accounting, so I accepted the job and worked hard. It wasn't long before my salary increased. My uncle once told me that if I would always do more work than I was paid for everything would be okay. That was great advice.

My 16 years in public accounting built a solid foundation for my future business ventures. Be passionate about your work and learn all you can about your job. Your experience and the skills you acquire will prepare you for the next step in your career.

Cultivate a strong work ethic. I want to emphasize this characteristic. It not only benefits your employer, but it also improves your character. Working hard and going the extra mile will set you apart from those who only do what is expected of them. Let a strong work ethic become part of who you are.

While working passionately at your job, maintaining balance in your life will be one of the biggest challenges that you will face. It's easy to get so focused on building your career that you become sidetracked from the important things like family, church, and your community. You need to take care of yourself by maintaining balance in the spiritual, physical, mental, and social areas of your life. Remember that relationships are more important than anything. You need to ask yourself on a regular basis if you're in danger of sacrificing your relationships for the sake of your career.

When I became co-owner of Schilling Enterprises, I spent day and night my first year working to save our companies from financial disaster. My life was definitely not balanced, but that wasn't new to me. When I was working at the accounting firm in Alabama, I worked long hours. I missed a lot of good times with my daughter Leslie while she was growing up. I am thankful that I've had the opportunity, hopefully, to make up for some of it. When you're wrong, you should learn from your mistakes and be wise enough to ask for forgiveness. I'm thankful for second chances.

Beth told me something long ago that has stuck with me. She said that I had better be good to her because she is the one who will stand beside me even if everyone else is gone. That still comforts me, and I'm thankful that Beth remains my best friend after 48 years of marriage.

Guard your relationships. Show your family you love them by spending quality time with them. They will love and respect you for it. Other people will observe your actions and respect you as well.

Another difficult but rewarding lesson is to put "first things" first. You must have the discipline to prioritize your choices. Relationships should be our highest priority.

Sometimes our most important relationships can conflict with each other. For example, in January, 2010, our family was preparing to travel to Los Angeles to see Barrett, my oldest grandson, play in the Rose Bowl at the NCAA Championship football game. Our family was very excited! Just then I received the news that my good friend and mentor of 30 years, Herbert Rhea, had passed away. I was faced with a dilemma. Should I go with my family to the game in California or should I stay home and attend my close friend's funeral? This was definitely an important decision because it was about relationships.

When I need wisdom I pray to God. I prayed for His wisdom and guidance in this situation. I believe He directed Beth and me to visit Herb's family at their home. Privately we expressed our sadness for their loss and to express our support for them. It was a great visit. At the end of our time with them, they encouraged us to go to the Championship Bowl. They said that Herb would want us to go.

I went to my grandson's game with peace in my heart because I knew I was doing the right thing at that particular time. How will you go about making decisions like this? If you face a dilemma, ask God for His wisdom and guidance. Then listen for His advice. You will be able to put first things first.

You will be faced with things in life that aren't interesting to you. They may be things that are hard to do, but if they are your responsibility, you must do them. By concentrating on the positive and following through to the best of your ability, you'll build integrity and mental toughness. This will help you do difficult things like taking care of a sick parent, for example. Who are you going to be when the tough times come?

Life Principle #2

Improve your mind continually.

IT'S IMPORTANT to keep your mind active. Be interested in different subjects that make you think. Read good books. Cultivate a desire to learn.

Grow your faith. In the midst of your busy life, make a point of having some quiet time alone every day, preferably in the morning. Control your thoughts. Don't let the bad thoughts in. If they do come in, put them out of your mind immediately. Use discipline to do the right things and think the right things. Live a principle-centered life.

Understand the difference between knowledge and wisdom. Make a point of being around people who make wise decisions. Think positively about life and be proactive. Don't wait for things to happen to you. Have a vision for what you want to do in life and pursue it with character and perseverance.

One of the most life-shaping things you can do is to find one or two mentors who will teach, help, and challenge you. How do you find a mentor? Typically, a mentor is someone who has experienced what you're going through currently. But more than that, a mentor is someone you respect based on their character and the way they conduct their lives. A mentor can only be meaningful to you if you follow their advice and example.

I have been fortunate to have had several mentors. When I moved to Memphis from Florence, Alabama, a mutual friend, Jesse Keller, introduced me to Herbert Rhea. For almost three decades I benefitted from Herbert's friendship and counsel, both in business and personal matters. I was blessed to have him for a mentor.

Jesse and Herbert had met a few years earlier when they worked together on the sale of a business whose home office was in Florence. Jesse was a mentor to me for over 50 years. We met at First Baptist Church in Florence. He was an attorney and a great friend. We worked together many times as we had several mutual clients. I was his CPA; he was my attorney.

Jesse loved Jesus and His church. He was a strong churchman and statesman who spoke and lived his convictions. He also loved history. He nicknamed me "Light Horse" after Robert E. Lee's dad, "Light Horse" Harry Lee. The nickname really fit me, because my name is Harry Lee Smith.

When Jesse died four years ago, Beth and I were in Florida. His wife Betty asked me to serve as a pallbearer. I didn't have the right clothes with me, so I bought a new suit, shirt, tie, and shoes, and I chartered a small plane to take us to Florence to attend the funeral. I still miss him today, as I did that day four years ago. Herbert and Jesse were two great friends and two great mentors.

In addition to finding a mentor, I also encourage you to find an accountability partner. This is someone who knows you well and will be completely honest with you. In my early days as a CPA, I saw men make compromises which led to failure and loss. I believe that a good accountability partner would have pointed out their bad decisions and warned them that they were headed for trouble. Having a mentor and an accountability partner will help you lay a foundation for honesty and integrity

One of the benefits of serving on boards is the opportunity to learn in-depth about different segments of business. For example, the years I served on The Med and Baptist Hospitals boards gave me an in-depth experience in health care. Serving on the University of Memphis Board of Visitors and the boards for Union University and Evangelical Christian School taught me about educational institutions. Serving on a bank board gave me an opportunity to learn about banking and the many ways it connects with the business world.

It takes a couple of years of board service before you can comprehend the intricacies of the business or institution. Learning about these complex organizations has exercised and continues to exercise my mind in a healthy, positive way.

To be successful in your career, you must continue to learn. One way is to make contacts in other cities with successful businesses like yours that are not your direct competitors. When I became president of the car dealerships, I understood the financial management aspect, but not all the internal operations. Most people who are promoted to key leadership positions have started from the bottom and learned each part of their business as they worked up through the organization. I, however, came in as president. Managers reported to me, but I lacked the experience and knowledge that is acquired over time.

I wanted to learn everything I could about the automobile business, so I went to cities like Atlanta to visit the Lincoln-Mercury dealerships there. I hired a taxi driver for the day as I made my visits. When I arrived at a dealership, I asked to see the owner or general manager. I introduced myself and asked if I could spend time with them. I told them I was new in the business and wanted to learn their philosophy of operating a car dealership. They were nice and helpful. When I was in St. Louis, Dallas, or other cities, I did the same thing. People are open to helping you if you will just ask. It was amazing how much I learned from them.

Once I flew to St. Petersburg, Florida, to visit the #1 Lincoln-Mercury dealership in the nation. I asked the owner, "Mr. Carlisle, how did you do it?" His answer was Pacific Institute, a leadership training program. Like all of us, Mr. Carlisle needed help, and he was smart enough to find someone to help him. The result was that his dealership was #1 in the nation.

Another time I visited the #1 dealer in Massachusetts. The owners of these dealerships took my visit as a compliment to their operational success. These visits were a great source of useful information for me. When I was a CPA, I advised clients to seek out those who were successful in their business and learn from them, but they usually didn't take my advice. When I had a chance to test my own advice as president of Schilling, I was happy to discover that it really did work.

God gives us good minds, but we need to use them to the best of our ability. When you intentionally exercise your mind, you'll discover creative ways of learning. As a result, you will grow both personally and professionally.

Life Principle #3

Live a lifestyle focused on good physical health.

WHEN I TURNED 50, I made some changes in my life. I knew I couldn't continue the way I was working and living. I sold some of our companies and promoted Rex, my son-in-law and partner, to be president of the Schilling automobile dealerships. Later, when we sold our last car dealership, Rex began working at Evangelical Christian School as the advancement director. He told me that his stress was greatly reduced in his new job.

When people asked me what was the hardest part of the automobile business, I answered without hesitation that it was dealing with the manufacturer. They understood one thing: selling cars. They referred to us as partners, but our goals were not always the same. They were interested in selling new cars regardless of the profit. They constantly pressured us to buy more cars (whether we needed more cars or not) and to spend too many dollars on advertising.

At Schilling, our goal was to sell new *and* used cars, along with providing service and parts sales for our customers. In the process, we made a good profit. Our efforts in areas other than new car sales sometimes seemed to irritate the manufacturer. When our new car sales were not what they thought they should be, the manufacturer's representatives increased the pressure on us. We had to be thick-skinned because the factory representatives rarely let up on the pressure. There was a district office in Memphis, so we saw a lot of the representatives as they came by our dealerships. We knew the manufactures were putting pressure on the representatives to sell us more new cars. As a result everyone was dealing with stress.

I wouldn't advise anyone to go through what Rex and I managed to work through. Some say there is such a thing as positive stress, but I can't believe that any stress is good for you. You have two choices in dealing with stress: learn to live with it or get away from it.

Stress is harmful to your health! It goes to the weakest part of your body. I was accustomed to trying to do 12 to 14 hours of work in 10 to 12 hours. I allowed my work to consume me and it almost did—literally. I had three bleeding ulcers before age 40.

Working 12 to 14 hour days was a standard part of my life even before becoming president of Schilling. As an accountant, I also developed two knots in the back of my neck from stress. I mentioned this recently when I was speaking to a group of accountants, and they laughed because they could relate to what I was saying. However, the mental, physical, and emotional effects of stress are no laughing matter, so do your best to keep it out of your life. Allow enough time to get your tasks done. Otherwise you will have to push too hard. Also, you should plan time for the unexpected. I'm thankful to say that my efforts to control the stress in my life resulted in the disappearance of those knots in my neck.

A few years ago Beth and I spent a week at the Pritikin Longevity Center in South Florida. We attended classes that taught us how important it is to eat healthy foods. They explained the negative impact of too much salt and sugar in our diet and the many ways it affects our bodies. They taught us the power of a combination of daily exercise and a good diet. We learned how to choose the right food and number of daily servings we should have. In today's busy world it's hard to maintain a healthy regimen on a regular basis, so a balanced diet and exercise should be our goal.

Eat well. Make healthy changes in your diet. Make physical exercise a priority or you will put it off. Consider getting a personal trainer. A professional trainer will ensure that you exercise properly and help you avoid injury. The trainer will be your accountability person. Try it and see if you don't accomplish more.

Studies have shown the importance of a positive attitude. Get quality sleep each night. Try to relax and have some fun as you go through life. Don't be too serious; laugh and enjoy life! Look for the best in everything.

Research shows that people who are spiritual heal faster than those who aren't. It is important to recognize our Creator and His love for us.

Life Principle #4

Practice ethical standards.

DEVELOP GOOD work ethics. Consider this question: How will I handle the "gray areas" of my profession and my life? A very wise man told me, "If there is a doubt, don't do it; but don't judge someone who does." I wish I had asked him that question a few years earlier. There were times in my early years in the automobile business that I probably didn't handle the gray areas as well as I should have. As time went by, I concentrated on improving the way I handled situations that fell into the gray areas. Our guiding principles at Schilling gave me a good framework to build on. When you make mistakes and compromise your principles, I assure you that the results will not be worth the cost.

In my accounting practice I discouraged clients from taking short cuts on their tax returns. I knew that whatever they saved in dollars would cost them more in lost sleep. I think this holds true for all short cuts we take. Being able to sleep soundly with a clear conscience is very rewarding. Unfortunately, it takes the aging process for some of us to learn how to handle these gray areas. But the important thing is that we do learn.

Never comprise your ethical standards. Many times big mistakes start as small mistakes. This is true in ethical comprises also. Sadly, too many times I have seen people fail when they seemed to have it all together. They became trapped in a work situation because their boss asked them to compromise. They have a large home to pay for, children to educate, and other bills to support their lifestyle. They think that they have no choice but to do what their boss tells them to do. But it's a trap, because they find out that one compromise leads to another. They lose something bigger than material things; they lose their integrity.

How do you know what is ethical or unethical? What is right or wrong is a core question that is answered from your soul. Most everyone has an innate sense of what is right or wrong in most every situation. If you struggle with questions of ethics, find a mentor and/or accountability partner—someone you think is living an ethical life. Let them help you examine your standards of ethics. This is a critical part of your future success in life.

Your conduct defines you when you're around other people. Your character defines you when you're by yourself. Our forefathers valued and practiced character. In America over the last 50 to 60 years, however, we have seen personality ethics overtake character ethics in the public arena.

You don't need to take short cuts to succeed. You want to build your character. If you do the harder right things and succeed because of your character and ethical standards rather than your personality, your success will leave a lasting mark on the world.

Courage is essential to having a code of ethics. You must have the courage to speak up when you disagree with the majority. Learn how to handle what I call "the 15-second rule." If someone makes a false statement about you, you have approximately ten to fifteen seconds to correct the statement or it becomes accepted as the truth. Don't be intimidated. Speak up and do what you think is right, even if it means being excluded.

Life Principle #5

Demonstrate a selfless attitude through humility.

I ONCE asked a man I admired very much, "What is the most important thing anyone can do to stay on the right track in life?" His answer was simple: "Humility."

If we live by that answer, we will strive to have an "abundance" mentality. That is, there is enough for everyone. Thinking that way will promote constructive rather than destructive competition. Some people have the idea, "If you gain, I lose," but it doesn't have to be that way.

Some people can't bring themselves to ask for help because they believe it is a sign of weakness. If a person would rather fail than ask for help, they are probably crippled by pride or insecurity. It takes humility and self-confidence to ask for help, but it is always a wise move. My goal in business was to succeed. I decided that I would rather succeed with someone's help than to fail. Asking for help is nothing to be ashamed of, because we all need help!

Use good manners. Be polite and courteous to people. Say "yes, sir" and "no, sir." Be on time for meetings. To be constantly late may seem arrogant and irresponsible, and it portrays a lack of interest and respect for others. Don't feel like you have to get even when you think someone has mistreated you. Things will work out in the long run. Take setbacks with grace and dignity. People will respect you for handling a tough situation graciously. Meekness is not weakness; it is strength under control.

Admit when you're wrong. Don't do things for self-promotion, but be the best you can be. We have heard that it is more blessed to give than to receive. Demonstrate that you value giving more than receiving. Recognizing a higher power in life should produce humility.

Pick your battles carefully. Everything does not have equal value. Some things are worth fighting for, but not all. During emotionally charged situations use your head, not your emotions, to guide your actions. Remember that nothing is usually gained by winning an argument. Try to understand others' situations without being judgmental.

If you practice a selfless attitude, there will be no job that is beneath you. At one of our car dealerships, I noticed paper towels lying on the restroom floor. I called the salespeople together and asked them, "Why don't you pick up paper towels when you see them on the floor? If everybody would help, we could all take responsibility for having our restroom floor clean." At a seminar in Louisville, Kentucky, I saw a church member helping the janitor by cleaning the restroom. We can all do things like that.

Once I was asked to pray at a teachers' luncheon for the Collierville schools. The school board members attended the event. I was wearing a tie but forgot to bring my coat with me. I felt a little underdressed for the occasion. I casually mentioned it to the school board members who were sitting at the table with me. One by one, they took off their coats and put them on the backs of their chairs. It showed that these men were willing to humble themselves and join me in my coatless-ness! Each day we have opportunities to practice humility and show respect for others.

Life Principle #6

Continually strengthen communication skills.

I CAN'T say it enough: Relationships are the most important thing in life. In every job and in every situation, you will be dealing with people. You need to strive to be forthright, tactfully honest, and transparent in your relationships. Be yourself. People will trust you if they understand who you are and recognize that you are authentic—you are who you say you are.

In the same way, you need to seek to understand others. Be honest with people. Tell them what you think, but always in a tactful way. Give them good feedback because they need it. When I first became president at Schilling, I would talk out my frustrations with Beth as we walked together in the evening. If your wife has good judgment, it can be very helpful to talk to her and listen to her advice.

When I was having a problem with a manager, Beth would say, "Have you confronted that person? You need to tell them what you're thinking. You owe it to them." I took her advice, and when I spoke to that person about what was bothering me, I discovered that they had been waiting for me to initiate the discussion. As an employee, do not be shy about asking your supervisor to discuss whatever is bothering you. Open discussions will build strong communication bridges between you and your supervisor. Then you will know exactly what your supervisor expects of you.

Avoid being judgmental of others. It's easy to misjudge what you think someone else is thinking or doing. Often we don't understand their motives or the reasons behind their behavior.

Dress well. You never get a second chance to make a good first impression. Apologize when you get off to a bad start with someone. Be a good listener. You will earn the right to have others listen to you. Use appropriate language. One of the lawyers we used at Schilling was an excellent attorney but had a habit of using bad language. I knew I needed to speak with him about it, so I tactfully approached him. I said, "You know, I don't believe that God will bless our companies if you use His name in vain." The attorney was completely receptive to what I said. He was not aware of his bad habit. He apologized and made a strong effort to break it.

Don't "burn bridges." Be nice to everyone. You never know when you'll need someone's help. On a flight to Atlanta with our Ford Motor Company district manager, I asked the gate attendant for directions to an ice cream shop in the airport. Kiddingly, he said, "Bring me some." I brought him an ice cream cone and he upgraded us to first class!

Never underestimate the positive effect of personal notes. I learned this from one of my partners in the CPA firm in Alabama who typed them on an old Underwood typewriter.

There will be times that you will need to speak up in a group meeting. While I served on the YMCA metro board, we were planning a fundraising event. Plans were being made to have an open bar and serve alcohol. Since young boys and girls were going to be at the event, I expressed concern about serving alcohol. It turned out that others were thinking the same thing. I'm thankful I had the courage to speak up because it changed the direction of the event.

If you need to improve your communication skills, get feedback from others. Ask people for suggestions. Go to workshops and seminars and read books on the subject. Your communication skills with others will be critical to your success.

Life Principle #7

Let your life reflect loyalty to others.

YOU WILL be rewarded for being loyal. People appreciate you when they know you will stick by them, especially in tough times. Over the years loyal friends have helped me through many unpleasant situations. I know from experience how important loyalty is, and I am always ready to help the people who have been loyal to me.

Practice loyalty in all areas of your life. Be loyal to your company, your supervisor, fellow employees, your friends, and your family. Don't say anything about anyone that you would mind him or her hearing. Not only can that be damaging to others, but it also reflects upon your character. Someone who talks about others in front of you will also talk about you in front of others.

When someone makes a false statement about another person, you have a responsibility to speak up. This takes courage, but it is a high form of loyalty to the person being slandered. It will also discourage people from making in-appropriate or false comments about others in front of you. That person will probably think twice before doing that again.

As humans, we all long to be understood and accepted. But being human, we often fail ourselves and others. Be sensitive when speaking to others, because you don't know what their struggles are. When possible, put someone in a positive rather than negative light. After all, you would want them to do the same for you.

Love your family and always be supportive of them. At work encourage your fellow employees and help them succeed. The worldly attitude is, "If they succeed, then I may not." This isn't right, because all can succeed! This is true in team sports. Teams with players who support and encourage their teammates win more. It is called teamwork.

Church is another place where loyalty is needed. Support your church leaders, both staff and lay members. Ministers especially need our loyalty and support. They have a challenging job and need to be appreciated and encouraged.

Boards of directors for profit and not-for-profit organizations need to support their companies' leadership. Employees need to see unified leadership between board members and management.

Life Principle #8

Develop leadership qualities.

GOOD LEADERS set an example for their employees and co-workers by working hard and being good role models. Synergy, or teamwork, is very important. Show people that you are interested in them and care for them. If you prove to your employees and co-workers that you appreciate their commitment and loyalty to the organization and that you are genuinely concerned about their welfare, you will find that they will follow you through good times and bad. A leader must earn respect. Respect is not a gift given to a person because they are in a leadership position. People will learn to trust you by the example you set.

Don't worry about who gets credit for good ideas; people will know what's really happening. The best leaders lead by serving others. Effective leaders are good followers first. I refer to them as "servant leaders." Be proactive and take the initiative by serving rather than waiting to be served. When you're upset, don't react immediately in words or actions. Wait until the next day when some of the heat of the moment has passed.

If you want to be an effective leader, do a job your own way. Don't try to do it like someone else would. The man who preceded me as president of Schilling Enterprises was Mr. Schilling's accountant. When Mr. Schilling died, he tried to manage the companies the way Mr. Schilling had done instead of managing in his own way. It didn't work.

In whatever job you have, do your best to make a positive difference. Understand that everyone needs encouragement. Look for opportunities to praise those around you. At Schilling we had a company chaplain who encouraged our employees. By stopping at our car dealerships once or twice a week, he got to know the people who worked there. He visited our employees and their families when they were sick and in the hospital, and he performed weddings and conducted funeral services. He would counsel with our employees in their homes.

Leaders have to make difficult decisions which impact the lives of other people. Sometimes a decision will not be popular with some of your staff, but it will be best for the majority. For example, when I became president of Schilling, the economy was bad and our companies were under extreme financial distress. To turn things around, I had to replace managers—most of whom were older than I was at the time.

One of those managers was a person I had known for a long time. I had a bleeding ulcer and was getting ready to leave to go the hospital when this man's wife called our home. She was upset about the decision I had made. Because of my physical condition Beth didn't want to let her talk to me. However, I knew that I would need to talk to her eventually, so I took the call. I listened as this lady told me very strongly how she felt about my decision to replace her husband. I was on my way to the hospital for treatment, but as the leader of our company I felt an obligation to let her speak her mind. Being the leader is not pleasant all the time, but to be effective you must be the leader all the time.

Rex and I knew that God owned our companies and trusted us to take care of them. That knowledge gave us the freedom to trust that the greatest Leader of all would guide us in our decisions. Sometimes we were guilty of taking back the ownership instead of remembering we were merely stewards. When we did, we exposed ourselves to the damaging effects of stress.

Practicing good leadership qualities will prepare you to be a leader in any situation. People will recognize your leadership skills and respect your work.

Life Principle #9

Strive to finish strong.

LIFE IS going to pass very quickly, so determine now how you will spend the time you are given. Strive to live a "no regrets" life. Give your life for the benefit of others if you want your life to count for something worthwhile.

Have you ever thought about writing a personal mission statement? Just like our guiding principles at Schilling helped us stay on track, your personal mission statement can help keep you on track.

I heard a story about a man who attended a funeral and discovered it was his own funeral! He was shocked to realize that people were going to stand up and talk about him. What were they going to say? Obviously that story is fiction, but it will help you think about how you want to be remembered. It will help you focus on the personal values you want to live by for the rest of your life.

It's one thing to know good and another thing to *do* good. Be a producer—not just a consumer. While you are here on earth live, learn, love, and leave a legacy. What will your legacy be? What is it about your life that you want to feel good about on your death bed? Will you be able to say that you lived a peaceful and happy life? What good will you leave behind?

Life can easily be swallowed up by chasing after "urgent" things. If we're not really careful about putting first things first, these urgent things will take the place of the truly important things. That means you'll have to master time management. You'll have to plan your week in advance and schedule the important things first. This might be a date with your wife, taking an employee to lunch, or supporting your child at a ballgame.

It's not easy to put first things first, but when you do, you'll be glad you did. Each day your relationships will be strengthened and enriched because you didn't let the urgent win out over the important.

Today there is a lot of talk about "networking." This can be a good tool if you genuinely care about other people. But sometimes people fall into the trap of *using* other people to get ahead in their careers. They believe they are taking a practical approach when they make connections that way, but they are missing something that is far more valuable than career advancement. Relationships are what really matter. As we live our day-to-day lives, we need relationships for support, encouragement, and friendship.

When my mentor Herbert Rhea died, someone at his church was preparing something to present to Herb's family. I was asked to send a note about my relationship with Herb and his impact on my life. Herb set an example for us all by living out the principles in this book, and he finished well. Speaking for many others who were influenced by him, here is what I said about my friend Herbert Rhea:

> I was blessed to know Herbert for almost 30 years. We were brought together by a mutual friend in Florence, Alabama. Herbert was a mentor, friend, and brother in Christ. He gave me both personal and business advice. He was a friend to my family and was respected by us. Herbert helped me buy and sell some of our businesses.

He had my overall business and personal affairs in his head and when we would meet, he could tell me what our goals were and would check on how these goals were progressing. His body was wearing down, but his mind was sharp right up to his last days.

I could say so many great things about my relationship with Herbert, but the best would be our spiritual relationship. We talked about our blessings, prayer requests and love for Christ. I watched him continue to grow spiritually and to come closer to Jesus as he grew older. I have a responsibility to pass along to others what Herbert has taught me and that is certainly one of my life goals.

Looking back on my four careers, I see that God brought people into my life to help and teach me. Maybe I haven't made the correct choice in every situation that I have faced, but I'm thankful for the lessons I've learned and the friendships I've made. I'm also thankful for the peace that God has given me in moving from one career to another.

That's one of the reasons I have written this book. I have been blessed by God and by others. Many have helped me by investing in my life. Now I want to give back to others by delivering these nine life principles to the next generation.

CONCLUSION

EXPERIENCE IS the world's greatest teacher, but the tuition is high. In my 68 years of living, loving, and making mistakes, I have attended the school of experience more than once. This school may be a harsh teacher, but learning and practicing these nine life principles may keep you from attending it very often.

Throughout this book I have stressed the importance of relationships. I believe that we cannot have full, meaningful, successful lives without the love and help of others. If you take one thing from this book, let it be the importance you should place on relationships.

How important are the relationships you have with God, family, friends and others? What are you doing to appreciate and improve your relationships? The most important relationship I have is my personal relationship with God, my heavenly Father, through His Son Jesus Christ. He created you and me to relate to Him and to each other. He wants us to know Him personally and to enjoy Him. With loving patience He waits for us to reach out to Him for help. Through Christ He offers us deliverance from the sin that condemns us and keeps us from being who He designed us to be. I am thankful for the assurance that when I die, I will spend eternity in heaven with Him. If you don't have that assurance, I hope that you will invite Jesus into your heart today and make Him Lord of your life.

My next most important relationship is with my family. My relationship with Beth, my wife, has been and is my most important earthly relationship. Although I had attended church all my life, when we married, Beth was more mature spiritually than I was. She has been a big factor in my spiritual growth. She has always been there for me, loving and supporting me in everything I have done. She's been very unselfish to share me with my work, church, and others. It means so much to me that she has always prayed for me and continues to pray for me every day. She is truly my best friend.

Also, my relationships with Leslie, Rex, Barrett, Harrison, and Walker are very important to me. I not only stress the importance of relationships to you, I try to live them personally every day. I continue to seek guidance and the wisdom to improve my relationships and to be open to new ones.

It has taken many years of experience to develop my nine principles. Your principles may be different from mine, but it is important for you to spend time working on a set of principles that you can use as guideposts. Remember, it is said, "If you don't stand for something, you will fall for anything." I hope that my nine principles will get you started on a path to develop your own principles and that you will distinguish yourself by your character and ethical standards.

Finally, do not let anyone tell you that living a Christian life will prevent you from being successful in the business world. I can tell you that the opposite is true. Throughout this book I have related actual events that I have faced and the help and guidance that I received from my relationship with God. As president of Schilling, when we were struggling to save our businesses, I remember saying, "If it were not for God, I don't know how I would make it!" We desperately needed someone to deliver us— to rescue us—from the danger of financial ruin. I knew that God was our only hope, and I put my trust in Him.

Psalm 91:15 says, "He will call on Me, and I will answer him. I will be with him in trouble. I will deliver him and honor him." God did deliver us from those troubles, and He had a plan to prosper our companies if we did things His way. I want to honor Him for His goodness and faithfulness to me throughout my life. It was true then, and it's true now: If it were not for God, I don't know how I would make it! He will do the same for you.

ABOUT THE AUTHOR

HARRY SMITH first showed his entrepreneurial spirit at the age of nine when he began delivering newspapers on a bicycle in his hometown of Florence, Alabama. Through his school years he expanded his paper routes and paid his way through college.

After graduating from the University of North Alabama, Harry spent 16 years as a CPA in Florence. In 1980, at the age of 37, he became co-owner and president of Schilling Enterprises in Memphis, Tennessee, a corporation with companies that included automobile dealerships, real estate, trucking, HVAC, and auto parts. In a struggling economy, Harry engineered a financial reversal that rescued the Schilling companies from bankruptcy and transformed them into profitable businesses.

Since selling the last of the companies in 2005, Harry has focused on giving back to the community by serving on for-profit and not-for-profit boards in the areas of health care, education, religion, manufacturing, transportation, and banking.

With his partner, Boyle Investment Company, Harry is developing 448 acres for mixed use in Collierville, Tennessee. He recently sold a saddle manufacturing company in Texas. At the University of Memphis, he serves as Executive-in-Residence at the Fogelman College of Business and Economics.

Harry has been married to Mary Elizabeth (Beth) Smith for 48 years. They have a daughter, Leslie, who is married to Rex Jones, and three grandsons: Barrett, Harrison, and Walker Jones. Barrett was on the University of Alabama football team that won the 2010 Bowl Championship Series title. Harry serves as a deacon at Bellevue Baptist Church. He holds an honorary doctorate from Union University in Jackson, Tennessee. In 2004 he was inducted into the Society of Entrepreneurs.

CPSIA information can be obtained at www.ICGtesting.com
Printed in the USA
LVOW011025190213

320652LV00003B/5/P